IMISCOE Research Series

This series is the official book series of IMISCOE, the largest network of excellence on migration and diversity in the world. It comprises publications which present empirical and theoretical research on different aspects of international migration. The authors are all specialists, and the publications a rich source of information for researchers and others involved in international migration studies.

The series is published under the editorial supervision of the IMISCOE Editorial Committee which includes leading scholars from all over Europe. The series, which contains more than eighty titles already, is internationally peer reviewed which ensures that the book published in this series continue to present excellent academic standards and scholarly quality. Most of the books are available open access.

For information on how to submit a book proposal, please visit: http://www.imiscoe.org/publications/how-to-submit-a-book-proposal.

More information about this series at http://www.springer.com/series/13502

Agnieszka Weinar
Amanda Klekowski von Koppenfels

Highly-Skilled Migration: Between Settlement and Mobility

IMISCOE Short Reader

Agnieszka Weinar
Institute of European and Russian Studies
Carleton University
Ottawa, ON, Canada

Amanda Klekowski von Koppenfels
Brussels School of International Studies
University of Kent
Etterbeek, Belgium

ISSN 2364-4087 ISSN 2364-4095 (electronic)
IMISCOE Research Series
ISBN 978-3-030-42203-5 ISBN 978-3-030-42204-2 (eBook)
https://doi.org/10.1007/978-3-030-42204-2

This Springer imprint is published by the registered company Springer Nature Switzerland AG.
The registered company address is: Gewerbestrasse 11, 6330 Cham, Switzerland

Contents

List of Boxes

Chapter 1
Introduction

1.1 Statement of Objectives

Simply put, migration is a politicized topic. This applies both to migration itself as well as post-migration integration, and is the case both in the Global North and the Global South. There are, of course, variations in the degree of politicization, but it remains broadly present. However, on the other hand, highly-skilled migrants are one group of migrants who are only rarely politicized or seen in a negative light, both in political and in public discourse (e.g. Heath and Richards 2018). Conventional wisdom has it that highly-skilled migrants are high-earners with needed skills and that they integrate easily and quickly. This perception makes them a "wanted" migration flow (Triadafilopoulos 2013). However, as with most migration flows, there is quite some distance between popular perceptions of this migration flow and the more nuanced picture uncovered by social research. The objective of this Reader is to provide a basic understanding of the migration of the highly-skilled, but also to raise questions and to contribute to closing the divide between popular perception and research-based findings. We should note that the publications we have worked with have been overwhelmingly written in English. We are aware of the wealth of literature in other languages, and hope that others will expand this review beyond the Anglophone works reviewed here. The Reader will thus provide an up-to-date review and critical analysis of literature on highly-skilled migration, within linguistic limits. The review will follow three broad axes of analysis: definition and conceptualization of highly skilled migration; integration of highly-skilled migrants; and emerging patterns of migration and mobility.

An attempt to define the term already raises questions. Also referred to as "highly-educated" or "highly-qualified" migrants, there is not one universally agreed-upon definition of the highly skilled migrant. The definitions vary depending on the source, country and context. In the political realm, some lawmakers define the highly-skilled by using a salary scale, while others use level of education

© The Author(s) 2020
A. Weinar, A. Klekowski von Koppenfels, *Highly-Skilled Migration:
Between Settlement and Mobility*, IMISCOE Research Series,
https://doi.org/10.1007/978-3-030-42204-2_1

(Chaloff and Lemaitre 2009). In the academic realm, the definition differs from author to author, with many authors not even defining the term at all. Where definitions are offered, there is, however, a broad consensus that the level of education, rather than the salary scale is the appropriate measure (Smith and Favell 2006; Triandafyllidou and Gropas 2014). The multi-causality of migration is, however, rarely recognized, with the indicator of education level rarely applied to such migrant categories as refugees or spouses, despite the fact that many of them meet the same criteria. We can then ask whether the definition of the "highly-skilled" migrant is limited to visa category, and not necessarily linked to an individual's skills? Very often in popular discussion, this is the case, resulting in a mischaracterization of migrants' profile, and further distorting the rhetoric surrounding migration and integration.

Students are a special category, considered highly-skilled in some cases, yet not in others (She and Wotherspoon 2013; Raghuram 2013). This then leaves us asking: what is it exactly that differentiates the highly-skilled migrant from simply a migrant?

In the Reader, we will delve deeper into the variety of experiences, discourses and realities of highly skilled migrants, focusing especially on geographical differences (Koser and Salt 1997). We divide our analysis into three groups of highly-skilled migrants, differentiated by region: North-North migrants, South-North migrants, and North-South migrants. Perhaps unsurprisingly, the first two groups will be more prominent in the analysis, not only because of their larger numbers (according to available figures) but also because of the rich literature on these groups; the third group, a more specific flow, will be discussed in less detail (Odok 2013). The North, here, is broadly conceptualized as being those countries which are members of the Organization for Economic Cooperation and Development (OECD). North-North migration might, then, be migration within the European Union, or from Canada or the United States to Europe, as well as the inverse.

These highly-skilled North-North migrants are, more often than not, however, characterized not as migrants *per se*, but as "expatriates," "lifestyle migrants" (Benson and O'Reilly 2009), "cosmopolitans" (Brimm 2010), "Eurostars" (Favell 2011), "elite migrants" (Beaverstock 2005) or as "knowledge migrants" (e.g. Ackers 2005). Although the term "corporate expatriate" is often used, we find that it is limiting; these specific postings and pay packages are also used outside of the corporate world, including by international NGOs and international organisations. For this reason, we prefer the term "organisational expatriate" and will use that throughout this Reader. At the same time, we note that the term "expatriate" is a very specific term, referring to those on time-limited deployment and specific pay and often tax packages. It has nonetheless become widely – erroneously – used to refer to all migrants from the Global North, and we will, in this Reader, demonstrate that the variety of migrants from the Global North includes the organisational expatriate, but is not limited to the organisational expatriate.

We find it of particular interest that North-North migrants are, for the most part, presented as non-migrants; as such, their integration is also often perceived as a separate phenomenon from that of "migrants". Here, too, we notice a distinction between highly-skilled migrants from the Global North and from the Global South. Those from the Global North seem to be exempt from the expectation of integration, with, indeed, self-segregation rather seen as being the norm (see, e.g. Ahmed 2011; Beaverstock 2002; Cohen 1977; Croucher 2009; Fechter 2007; Glasze 2006; Pow 2011; Smith and Favell 2006). Highly-skilled migrants from the Global South, on the other hand, face a different set of challenges and expectations (Lowell and Findlay 2001; Purkayastha 2005). Even though integration of those from the Global South is often implicitly assumed to be smoother than that of their lesser-skilled compatriots, their experiences are nonetheless often closer to the experience of the low-skilled migrant than the idealized highly-skilled path to integration.

This bifurcated view of highly-skilled migrants can be understood by a view through the lens of "country labels". The "country labels" can be operationalized as the effects of the country of origin (Klekowski von Koppenfels and Weinar 2019). These effects are discussed as endogenous or exogenous features. The characteristics that are endogenous to the country are not mere perceptions, they are rather components of a migrant's human capital. These components can underpin a "country label" but are measurable, such as level and quality of education, social and cultural development, or measurement of migrants' health. The characteristics exogenous to the country, or what might be called the "country label", is a set of beliefs existing in any given host country vis-à-vis a country of origin and its citizens. These beliefs can result in negative stereotypes and racism in the host country towards one group, but also in ungrounded overtly positive attitudes towards another group, **regardless of the migrant's skill level**. These labels are important factors that support or challenge integration.

In our second axis of analysis, integration, there has been substantial literature on specific patterns of integration among highly-skilled migrants (Nohl et al. 2014; Duchêne-Lacroix and Koukoutsaki-Monnier 2016; Ryan and Mulholland 2014; Raghuram 2013; Piekut 2013; Fechter and Walsh 2010; Fechter 2007), but an examination of the integration of these migrants *as migrants* is still lacking. The migration of highly-skilled migrants is often portrayed as a movement other than migration, and their integration is similarly often portrayed as a phenomenon separate from that of the low-skilled migrants. When discussing highly skilled migration, Smith and Favell (2006) argued that integration policy seems to be thought unnecessary for this category of migrants. Yet, we point out here, integration is a challenge for all migrants, regardless of skill level. Indeed, highly-skilled migrants are still newcomers to a society and - aside from those recruited externally for positions - they also face barriers to the labour market, including recognition of qualifications, and obstacles in cultural integration. Also, the highly-skilled are the very group that most often experiences employment below their skill level, loss of status and painful adjustment trajectories, which also seem to be exacerbated for female migrants (Gauthier 2016; Adamuti-Trache 2011; Purkayastha 2005).

The migration trajectories and possible success of highly skilled migrants are shaped by several factors that can be applied to any migration flow and have been discussed in literature: the way they enter a country (with a job offer or not); marketability of skills that they have (in the IT sector or other sectors) and existence of strong networks (Zikic et al. 2010; Mahroum 2000). In addition, the highly-skilled compete for jobs with highly-skilled natives, a competition which is said to be fiercer than the one on lower skill levels (Cantwell 2011; Schuster et al. 2013). The policy context is also crucial: intra-EU movers face fewer hurdles to their integration than transatlantic movers. The lower-skilled face higher integration challenges than the highly-skilled. However, the highly skilled face considerable integration challenges as well; in assuming that only the lower-skilled face challenges, the highly-skilled are hurt: integration support in the host countries focuses on low-skilled immigration and the highly-skilled are often left to their own devices to create a life on their own (Buzdugan and Halli 2009; She and Wotherspoon 2013). This can include painful transitions for trailing spouses - who often do not have the right to work - and children. Arguably, however, integration seems to be more difficult in the case of South-North migration, often because of the racial or cultural contexts in which migrants find themselves. As some researchers attest, the same challenges are part and parcel of North-South migration (Camenisch and Suter 2019). These migrants are usually inserted in a labour market but live in an international bubble that makes any meaningful integration impossible (Lauring and Selmer 2010), with negative consequences for themselves and their families.

The last axis of analysis is the evolving pattern of brain flows. Over the last two decades, the migration of the highly-skilled has become more fluid. It is no longer necessarily a migration for settlement, but often mobility to facilitate a job-hunt. Again, it seems that the North-North experience is distinct from that of South-North migration. For example, we are now experiencing a fundamental change in the transatlantic migration system, which is arguably a truly complete system of mobility, with circular and temporary mobility as the predominant model for transatlantic flows of people (Harpaz 2019, 2015; Weinar 2017; Cairns 2014; Chalk 2014). This change has to be critically examined: the factors facilitating circularity and temporariness depend on policies at both origin and destination, on the mobility opportunities offered at both ends of the migration system (e.g. bilateral temporary mobility schemes, academic and research cooperation, business cooperation) as well as the possibilities offered by one's passport (Pellerin 2011). Mobility also reflects the circulation of skills across the Atlantic, as well as circulation of labour, both encouraged by specific trade arrangements and a variety of bilateral or multilateral cooperation tools (Hübner 2011; Pellerin 2017). Indeed, it has been argued that highly-skilled migrants from countries which bestow more mobility opportunities on its citizens (e.g. North-Western European countries) are not tied to their immigration decision and if they do not reach their goals overseas, they have the choice of returning or moving elsewhere (Weinar 2019; Camenisch and Suter 2019). Such mobility patterns are also more acceptable now than they were in the past, e.g. thanks to the increased acceptance of dual nationality and internationalization of skills (Harvey 2012). This experience is not, however, shared by South-North highly-skilled migrants, whose passports do not give them the same access to mobility (Harpaz 2019). Indeed, the patterns of South-North highly-skilled migrants remain more settlement-bound, which brings us back again to the distinction in integration between the highly-skilled migrants from the Global North and from the Global South.

Overall, this Reader seeks to draft the state-of-play in research on highly-skilled migration in the twenty-first century through a critical lens. Understanding the challenges of highly-skilled migration is increasingly important, as countries engage more strongly with specific immigration programs targeting this group. The rise of the highly-skilled middle class as well as lower barriers to mobility for educated professionals will likely boost the flows of this category of migrants. Indeed, the more human capital the world produces in a more mobile framework, the more highly-skilled migrants will be on the move, increasingly challenging our current understanding of drivers of migration, integration and belonging.

1.2 Organisation of the Book

The book is organised as follows. In the next chapter (Chap. 2) we discuss the definition of highly skilled migrants. We go through the main definitions of highly skilled migrants, both policy-applied definitions as well as the more academic. The chapter further discusses the variety of definitions and conceptualizations of highly skilled migrants, taking into account country of origin, gender and career path. We reflect upon the challenges policy makers and researchers face when trying to set boundaries of this particular category of migrants and present some of the critiques of the existing attempts of conceptualisation. We conclude that predominant academic discourses on highly skilled migration have been influenced by the public policy needs, and thus it is still the state and state administration – which approves visas – that has the final say in defining who counts as a highly skilled migrant or not.

Following from there, in Chap. 3, we discuss the relationship between the state and the highly skilled migrant. It starts with the critical discussion of policies and politics of highly skilled migration by examining the differences in hard and soft barriers to the full access to several measures of integration: labour market, citizenship, language and education. Using the conceptual framework of analysis built around macro- and meso-levels of integration, we look at the ways highly skilled migrants navigate labour market integration challenges. We put emphasis on the differences between experiences of migrants from the Global North and the South, and we discuss not only immigration experiences, but also return migration. The chapter continues with an overview of issues surrounding social and cultural integration. It also critically discusses the role of gender in highly skilled migration.

In Chap. 4, we propose to look deeper into the specific case of these Global Northerners who migrate within the Global North. As explained above, their experience is generally considered to be "non-migration". In the light of the recent research, we disagree with this consideration, and propose instead to use the case of North-North migration as an illustration of the complexities of highly skilled migration. We are interested in exposing factors common to all migrants, which impact the lives of even those who are privileged to be highly-skilled and mobile in the extremely open trans-Atlantic mobility space. At the heart of our discussion is an examination of the tension between settlement and mobility. We expand on the case of contemporary twenty-first century transatlantic migration system as model from which other migration systems might learn. We look into how policies in non-immigration domains (such as trade or education) can open up the space of circulation and how large-scale migrations can become associated with enhanced mobility, rather than with a domain of immigration policies. This mobility is however not a one-way or simple migration, as more freedom of movement lowers risks and brings more choices. While we might think, on the one hand, Global North transatlantic migrants might have an easier time migrating than do Global Southerners, on the other hand, they might also find integration difficult and, like Southerners as well, subsequently return. Integration challenges, often related to patterns of settlement and mobility, define North-North migration as much as any other migration. In our view, the Global North translatlantic case can thus enable broader generalisation about the experience of the highly skilled migrants.

We conclude with a review of the main concepts and themes of the book, and offer a research agenda for the future.

References

Ackers, L. (2005). Moving people and knowledge: Scientific mobility in the European Union. *International Migration, 43*(5), 99–131.

Adamuti-Trache, M. (2011). First 4 years in Canada: Post-secondary education pathways of highly educated immigrants. *Journal of International Migration and Integration/Revue de L'integration et de La Migration Internationale, 12*(1), 61–83.

Ahmed, A. (2011). Belonging out of context: The intersection of place, networks and ethnic identity among retired British migrants living in the Costa Blanca. *Journal of Identity and Migration Studies, 5*(2), 2–19.

Beaverstock, J. V. (2002). Transnational elites in global cities: British expatriates in Singapore's financial district. *Geoforum, 33*(4), 525–538.

Beaverstock, J. V. (2005). Transnational elites in the city: British highly-skilled inter-company transferees in New York City's financial district. *Journal of Ethnic and Migration Studies, 31*(2), 245–268.

Benson, M., & O'Reilly, K. (2009). Migration and the search for a better way of life: A critical exploration of lifestyle migration. *The Sociological Review, 57*(4), 608–625.

Brimm, L. (2010). *Global cosmopolitans: The creative edge of difference.* Springer.

Buzdugan, R., & Halli, S. S. (2009). Labor market experiences of Canadian immigrants with focus on foreign education and experience. *International Migration Review, 43*(2), 366–386.

Cairns, D. (2014). *Youth transitions, international student mobility and spatial reflexivity: Being Mobile? London.* New York: Palgrave Macmillan.

Camenisch, A., & Suter, B. (2019). European migrant professionals in Chinese global cities: A diversified labour market integration. *International Migration, 57*(3), 208–221.

Cantwell, B. (2011). Transnational mobility and international academic employment: Gatekeeping in an academic competition arena. *Minerva, 49*(4), 425–445.

Chalk, B. (2014). *Modernism and mobility: The passport and cosmopolitan experience*. London: Springer.

Chaloff, J., & Lemaitre, G. (2009). *Managing highly-skilled labour migration*.

Cohen, E. (1977). Expatriate communities. *Current Sociology, 24*(3), 5–90.

Croucher, S. (2009). Migrants of privilege: The political transnationalism of Americans in Mexico. *Identities: Global Studies in Culture and Power, 16*(4), 463–491.

Duchêne-Lacroix, C., & Koukoutsaki-Monnier, A. (2016). Mapping the social space of transnational migrants on the basis of their (supra) national belongings: The case of French citizens in Berlin. *Identities, 23*(2), 136–154.

Favell, A. (2011). *Eurostars and eurocities: Free movement and mobility in an integrating Europe* (Vol. 56). Somerset: John Wiley & Sons.

Fechter, A.-M. (2007). In V. Amit (Ed.), *In going first class?: New approaches to privileged travel and movement*. Berghahn Books.

Fechter, A.-M., & Walsh, K. (2010). Examining 'expatriate' continuities: Postcolonial approaches to mobile professionals. *Journal of Ethnic and Migration Studies, 36*(8), 1197–1210.

Gauthier, C.-A. (2016). Obstacles to socioeconomic integration of highly-skilled immigrant women: Lessons from Quebec Interculturalism and implications for diversity management. *Equality, Diversity and Inclusion: An International Journal, 35*(1), 17–30.

Glasze, G. (2006). Segregation and seclusion: The case of compounds for western expatriates in Saudi Arabia. *Geo Journal, 66*(1–2), 83–88.

Harpaz, Y. (2015). Ancestry into opportunity: How global inequality drives demand for long-distance European Union citizenship. *Journal of Ethnic and Migration Studies, 41*(13), 2081–2104.

Harpaz, Y. (2019). Compensatory citizenship: Dual nationality as a strategy of global upward mobility. *Journal of Ethnic and Migration Studies, 45*(6), 897–916.

Harvey, W. (2012). Brain circulation to the UK? Knowledge and investment flows from highly skilled British expatriates in Vancouver. *Journal of Management Development, 31*(2), 173–186.

Heath, A., & Richards, L. (2018). *How do Europeans differ in their attitudes to immigration? Findings from the European social survey 2002/03–2016/17* (OECD Social, Employment and Migration Working Papers No. 222). Paris: OECD.

Hübner, K. (2011). *Europe, Canada and the comprehensive economic and trade agreement* (Routledge Studies in Governance and Change in the Global Era 8). London/New York: Routledge.

King, R., & Raghuram, P. (2013). International student migration: Mapping the field and new research agendas. *Population, Space and Place, 19*(2), 127–137.

Klekowski von Koppenfels, A. & Weinar, A.. (2019). Forthcoming. Migration, mobility, integration, segregation – Migrations within the global north, introduction to the special section of *International Migration*.

Koser, K., & Salt, J. (1997). The geography of highly skilled international migration. *Population, Space and Place, 3*(4), 285–303.

Lauring, J., & Selmer, J. (2010). The supportive expatriate spouse: An ethnographic study of spouse involvement in expatriate careers. *International Business Review, 19*(1), 59–69.

Lowell, B. L., & Findlay, A. (2001). Migration of highly skilled persons from developing countries: Impact and policy responses. *International Migration Papers, 44*, 25.

Mahroum, S. (2000). Highly skilled globetrotters: Mapping the international migration of human capital. *R&D Management, 30*(1), 23–32.

Nohl, A.-M., Schittenhelm, K., Schmidtke, O., & Weiss, A. (2014). *Work in transition: Cultural capital and highly skilled migrants' passages into the labour market*. University of Toronto Press.

Odok, G. E. 2013. North–South migration. *The Encyclopedia of Global Human Migration*.

Pellerin, H. (2011). De La Migration à La Mobilité: Changement de Paradigme Dans La Gestion Migratoire. Le Cas Du Canada. *Revue Européenne Des Migrations Internationales, 27*(2), 57–75.

Pellerin, H. (2017). States and the management of the international mobility highly skilled labour in the age of Neoliberalism. *International Journal of Migration and Border Studies, 3*(4), 352–367.

Piekut, A. (2013). 'You've got Starbucks and coffee heaven... I can do this!' Spaces of social adaptation of highly skilled migrants in Warsaw. *Central and Eastern European Migration Review, 2*(1), 117–138.

Pow, C.-P. (2011). Living it up: Super-rich enclave and transnational elite urbanism in Singapore. *Geoforum, 42*(3), 382–393.

Purkayastha, B. (2005). Skilled migration and cumulative disadvantage: The case of highly qualified Asian Indian immigrant women in the US. *Geoforum, 36*(2), 181–196.

Raghuram, P. (2013). Theorising the spaces of student migration. *Population, Space and Place, 19*(2), 138–154.

Ryan, L., & Mulholland, J. (2014). 'Wives are the route to social life': An analysis of family life and networking amongst highly skilled migrants in London. *Sociology, 48*(2), 251–267. https://doi.org/10.1177/0038038512475109.

Schuster, A., Vincenza Desiderio, M., & Urso, G. (2013). *Recognition of qualifications and competences of migrants*. Belgium: International Organization for Migration Brussels.

She, Q., & Wotherspoon, T. (2013). International student mobility and highly skilled migration: A comparative study of Canada, the United States, and the United Kingdom. *Springerplus, 2*(1), 132.

Smith, M. P., & Favell, A. (2006). *The human face of global mobility: International highly skilled migartion in Europe, North America and the Asia-Pacific* (Vol. 8). Transaction Publishers.

Triadafilopoulos, T. (2013). *Wanted and welcome?: Policies for highly skilled immigrants in comparative perspective*. New York: Springer Science & Business Media.

Triandafyllidou, A., & Gropas, R. (2014). 'Voting with their feet' highly skilled emigrants from southern Europe. *American Behavioral Scientist, 58*(12), 1614–1633.

Weinar, A. (2017). From emigrants to free movers: Whither European emigration and diaspora policy? *Journal of Ethnic and Migration Studies, 43*(13), 1–19.

Weinar, A. (2019). European citizenship and identity outside of the European Union. In *London*. New York: Routledge.

Zikic, J., Bonache, J., & Cerdin, J.-L. (2010). Crossing national boundaries: A typology of qualified immigrants' career orientations. *Journal of Organizational Behavior, 31*(5), 667–686.

Chapter 2
Highly Skilled Migration: Concept and Definitions

2.1 Introduction

While there may be broad agreement on their desirability, there is not one agreed-upon definition of the highly-skilled migrant; the boundaries of the concept fluctuate depending on who is talking: economists favour a different approach than sociologists, while policymakers might have yet another view. In this chapter we will consider the various definitions of the highly skilled. Above all, we will look at two key factors drawn on in establishing these definitions: first, who sets the boundaries of the definition? Second, what is the purpose of any given definition? We will also address a number of inconsistencies in the definitions and conceptual frameworks which are used, and will present critical views of these conceptualisations.

But, first, we must acknowledge an important caveat: in the phrase "highly-skilled international migrant", it is the "international migrant" which remains the key term, with "international" an implicit part of the phrase. It means that these individuals are subject to national immigration policy and law. They often enjoy easier access to an entry visa and/or residence permit than their lower-skilled brethren, but none of them is exempt from these requirements. As all highly-skilled migrants are first and foremost individuals crossing international borders and therefore seeking to enter another nation-state, we thus need to look first at states' emigration and immigration policy. Indeed, our first, almost intuitive, answer to the question of who defines a highly skilled migrant is quite simple: the state does. The sovereign state exercises control over its borders; as such, it is up to the state to define who can enter, and under which rules – in short, to establish the definition of a migrant (Brettell and Hollifield 2014; Zolberg 1999; Weiner 1995).

The state sets the rules of entry through establishing visa categories and eligibility criteria for those categories, which, in turn, means that the state also ultimately defines the way data are collected. The means of data gathering thus additionally influences the ways in which the concepts of skills, education and migration are

© The Author(s) 2020
A. Weinar, A. Klekowski von Koppenfels, *Highly-Skilled Migration: Between Settlement and Mobility*, IMISCOE Research Series, https://doi.org/10.1007/978-3-030-42204-2_2

reflected in the datasets used by researchers. We may of course argue that the international legal framework has influenced many states' decisions in this field (Joppke 1999; Lavenex 1999; Soysal 1994), but ultimately a state is bound by the international order (only) as long as it chooses to be so bound (Krasner 2009; Checkel 1997; McSweeney 1999). The state is the real power-wielder as regards conceptualisation of highly skilled migrants when granting them entry to its territory either through specific highly-skilled immigration streams or programs for economic migration. Phrases such as "the best and the brightest," "international talent" and "chosen immigration" fill policy discourses and shape real-world migration streams.

Of course, not all highly skilled migrants come through the streams dedicated to this category – they may enter as spouses or as refugees, for instance – and this is where the state-driven conceptualisation can be contested. However, scholars studying migration largely follow the state-centred view of highly-skilled migrants, working within state-defined policy and visa categories, which continues to influence the shaping of the definition. When defining highly skilled migrants, the academic literature overwhelmingly perpetuates the educational, skill and income criteria within a labour-market oriented view of this migration flow. Only recently have some researchers begun to question this dominant approach (Raghuram 2013; van Bochove and Engbersen 2015) by broadening the categories of entrants who may be considered as highly skilled.

In the next sections of this chapter we examine the academic and policy debates on the meaning of "highly skilled migrant" from the state perspective. We cover the three criteria most often used in literature to specify who may be categorized as a highly skilled migrant, namely education, skills and income. In the second part of the chapter, we will discuss scholarship contesting these criteria and offering a more nuanced view of the highly skilled migrant.

2.2 Highly-Skilled Migrants as Workers

Who is the highly skilled migrant? In migration studies scholarship, highly skilled migration refers generally to the stream of migrant, i.e. foreign workers sharing specific characteristics and who therefore qualify for a particular visa category. More detailed definitions depend largely on the function of the research. A review of academic literature indicates that there is no consistent definition or measurement of highly skilled, for a variety of reasons, the principle being that the variety of conceptualisations that are used are not necessarily to be found in available data.

Scholars studying the highly-skilled as a group and interested in their outcomes on the labour market generally use a data-driven definition. Those interested in policies on highly skilled migration, on the other hand, tend to employ policy-driven definitions, while, finally, those scholars who are interested in the lived experience of educated migrants tend to contest the dominant conceptualisations. In what follows, we will present these approaches in more detail.

2.2.1 Data-Driven Research on Highly-Skilled

The most obvious starting place to define highly skilled is either by the level of education (Borjas 2005; Docquier and Marfouk 2006; Peri and Sparber 2011) or by classification of occupation (Bouvier and Simcox 1995; Espenshade et al. 2001; Libaers 2014). The basic definition, often used by economists as a proxy to narrow down the data for analysis, is that a highly skilled migrant is a person with tertiary (university-level) education. However, even this is not a simple measure: in his report to the United Nations on highly skilled migration, Lindsay Lowell noted that capturing educational level in the data is in itself tricky. He gives the example of the data collection that uses age proxy: tertiary education should be normally captured in the adult group over 25, while most of the measures using age proxy focus on general cohort of 15+ (Lowell 2005). Building on this observation, Ron Skeldon noted in 2018 that the OECD, when discussing highly skilled in its latest publication, was basing its analyses on the population who are 15 years of age and over, thus including the population currently in secondary and in higher education (Skeldon 2018; Dumont and Lemaître 2005). This inclusion underestimates the highly skilled population and potentially leads to skewed data. However, this approach is a particular one, and the most common definition of highly skilled tends to be limited to persons with "tertiary" education, typically meaning a formal two-year college degree or more. Lowell notes that, as tertiary education is "the most readily available international statistic", it becomes the default measure for the highly skilled (2005, p. 2). This approach focusing on educational attainment is often used by economists, with the highly skilled can thus more easily identified within a larger sample of migrants. This variable has been widely used among those studying the effects of emigration on the countries of origin, and in particular "brain drain" (see Chap. 3).

Development economists interested in questions of brain drain have used data sets on international skilled migration, which defined skilled immigrants as foreign-born workers with university or post-secondary training (Carrington and Detragiache 1998; Adams 2003; Docquier and Marfouk 2006). In the same area of development studies, Beine and his colleagues concluded that existing databases did not differentiate enough between student migrants, i.e. those who came to gain education, and migrant workers, i.e. those who came with a certain level of education already obtained in the country of origin. They thus constructed a database which uses immigrants' age of entry to the country of destination as a proxy for where education was acquired. This distinction was important for the analysis of the effects of highly skilled migration on the country of origin (Beine et al. 2007). With time, the database has been used for a variety of studies, almost always focusing on the country of origin (Docquier and Rapoport 2012; Docquier et al. 2009; Rapoport et al. 2011; Beine et al. 2008).

Yet, the perspective of the country of destination requires a different set of definitions and, consequently, data. Many scholars employ the definitions proposed by the OECD, which tend to mix educational attainment with occupation. In the 1990s, OECD identified highly-skilled as meaning that an individual has a university degree or extensive/ equivalent experience in a given field (OECD 1998). At that time, this included "highly skilled specialists, independent executives and senior managers, specialized technicians or tradespersons, investors, business persons, "keyworkers", and sub-contract workers" (OECD 1998, p. 21). This mixed approach brings to light the occupational dimension of highly skilled, acknowledging that not all skilled migrants actually work as such in their host countries. Some scholars have developed the occupation-based definition further. Czaika and Parson propose that any migrant with occupational qualifications in the top three categories of the International Standard Classification of Occupations (ISCO) should be considered a skilled migrant (Czaika and Parsons 2017). This approach is then tested on ten national administrative datasets. This comparative approach has been adopted by scholars studying particular occupations (Clemens and Pettersson 2008; Bhargava et al. 2011; Franzoni et al. 2012; Czaika and Toma 2017). Yet, as Boucher noted., "Such benchmarking exercises may be driven primarily by pragmatism and a concern to draw large-scale cross-national comparative inferences even if they are not situated within the real effects of immigration selection policies" (2019, p. 14).

Most governments define, and thus measure, highly skilled immigrants in terms of both education and occupation. For example, the United States' well known H-1B visa is based on a list of occupations and a minimum degree requirement of a baccalaureate (4-year US bachelor's degree) or equivalent (Lowell 2001; McLaughlan and Salt 2002). Scholars of public policy, on the other hand, conceptualise the highly skilled through the notion of "skills." This preference responds to the clear utilitarian view of highly-skilled migrants, notably as vessels of specific knowledge and competences; much scholarship refers to them as "skills" or "human capital" (Dzvimbo 2003; Ganguli 2014; Mahroum 1999; Cunha and Heckman 2007; Becker 1975 Box 2.1).

Box 2.1: Highly Skilled Migrants in the US
Known as a classic immigration country, the United States is better known for a focus on family in permanent migration – including parents, siblings, aunts, uncles and cousins as well as children and spouses – rather than labor migration. However, when it comes to temporary migration, labor migration comes to the fore.

The H-1B visa, established in 1990, is the best-known highly-skilled worker visa in the US, issued for 3 years and renewable once; H-1B visa holders can transition to permanent (Green Card) status. The cap on the H-1B, set annually by Congress, has remained at 65,000 since 2005, with an additional 20,000 for those with a minimum of an MA from a US university. In response to employer demand, it was raised to 115,000 in 1999 and 2000 and 195,000 for 2001–2003, but returned to 65,000 in 2004. Many employers are exempt from the H-1B, with the result that 570,000 migrants entered the US in 2018 on H-1B visas. The H-1B is just one of over 20 visa categories, however, many of which would also be seen as highly skilled, such as O-1 "Individuals with Extraordinary Ability or Achievement". Organisational expatriates are here in a separate category, L-1A "Intracompany Transferee Executive or Manager" and related visas – accounting together for nearly one million non-immigrant admissions in 2018.

Another way in which data on the highly skilled are collected is to use wage level as a proxy for skills and education. George Borjas introduced this concept, asserting that migrants and natives with the same skills are perfect substitutes in a receiving country's labour market (Borjas 2005). He also suggested that skills can be measured by income level. Recognizing that migration flows represent a continuum of skills and income levels rather than distinct categories, he proposed to set a cut-off line at a certain income level, proposing that the highly skilled migrants were those above this cut-off line. In his view, the value of the same skill would be reflected similarly across countries, because employers would, he argued, always recognize the net worth of such skilled workers, also rendering datasets comparable (Borjas 1987). Some scholars took on this idea and in some publications, wages are indeed seen as a proxy for "skill." Indeed, Ruggles and colleagues have gone so far as to develop a dataset that considers both occupation and salary (Ruggles et al. 2010). However, this approach has not been widely used in publications on the highly skilled in migration studies, in contrast to public policies themselves. Salary, bound together with educational attainment, has been at the core of the definition of highly skilled for several migration policies, e.g. European Union Blue Card, which adopts educational criteria as well as wage criteria (Cerna 2013; Triandafyllidou and Isaakyan 2014).

The difficulty of determining a clearly defined category of the highly skilled, from the point of view of a receiving country and its system of data collection, has been pointed out recently by Parsons et al. (2014). They presented three perspectives on the conceptualisation of highly skilled migration: definitions in national immigration statistics; definitions that govern national occupational nomenclatures, and definitions used in unilateral immigration policies. They identified three major discordances. First, a definitional discordance, when the same individual may be defined as highly skilled or not depending upon the variables used to capture them in data collection (e.g. tertiary education defined as 2-year college education or Master's degree). Second, an occupational discordance, when the same individual may be classified as highly skilled or not depending upon the occupational classification applied to them (e.g. national occupational grids (NOC)). And third, a policy discordance when migrants defined as such and working in the same occupations may be considered as highly skilled or not depending on the immigration policy stream through which they have entered (e.g. highly skilled, refugees or spouses) (Parsons et al. 2014). This inconsistency throughout data, methodologies and policy choices affects many individuals who are not identified – or counted – as highly skilled migrant workers (de Haas et al. 2018; Pethe 2007).

2.2.2   The Notion of "Skill"

As noted in the introduction to this chapter, immigrant categories are defined by the interest of the state: the current needs of the labour market as well as other economic and social concerns. Many authors have noted that "highly skilled" has, over the years, become a synonym of desired, unproblematic migration (Triadafilopoulos 2013; Bielewska 2018; Beaverstock 2005; Iredale and Appleyard 2001; Boucher 2019; McLaughlan and Salt 2002; Raghuram 2004). Those who enter through skilled visa streams defined by educational attainment are often viewed as facing fewer challenges to integration and thus being less of a burden to the welfare state. As noted, however, there does remain a distinction for migrants from the Global South, for whom tertiary education is assumed to facilitate integration, and for those from the Global North, for whom integration is often not expected. Most importantly, members of the public seem to believe that the skilled migrants fill in a gap on the labour market and are less likely to replace domestic workers, thus not representing direct competition (Naumann et al. 2018; Kerr et al. 2016). One consistent element of these discourses is that the "skill" is clearly definable and easily differentiated from "unskilled" or "low-skilled" labour migration.

As noted in the previous subsection, there is considerable variation on how the highly skilled are identified in a policy context. Yet even the variation presented above only represents one broad category of the highly skilled. "Skill" is context-related and socially-constructed (e.g. Skeldon 2018). The term "skilled" can be broader or narrower than a college or university degree. For example, athletes and artists are, depending on the receiving country, often considered to be highly skilled but they do not necessarily hold a tertiary degree. Most importantly, the term "highly skilled" defined by educational attainment excludes many people with vocational education: this can relate to welders as well as some categories of health care practitioners. At the same time, both welding and health care professions top the lists of the migrants who are recruited in many labour immigration programs (Green and Green 1995; Beach et al. 2007; Walsh 2008).

To align the academic data-driven definitions with the real-world policy-making outcomes (which, in turn, create the administrative data upon which scholars base their analyses), public policy and migration studies literature focuses on the "marketable skill"-centered definition of the highly skilled. While not lending itself toward easy conceptualization in terms of data, it has been the most widely used in the research geared toward policy analysis. First prominent attempts to conceptualise highly-skilled migration around skills and the interest of the receiving labour market appeared in the 1990s. In that time the question of defining the highly skilled began to emerge, and it revolved around one question: what is the utility of the migrant worker? If they were needed because of their high skills, they were, indeed, highly skilled, leading to a somewhat circular definition. In this context the occupation and actual employment of the migrant seemed to be the more important dimension of the definition. For example, Salt (1997) noted that expansion of industries and services drove a growing recognition of the importance of international recruitment and mobility of the highly skilled in the 1990s. This expansion could only be supported by the increased employment of human talent with very specific skills. If these skills were not available locally, the companies would push for a greater opening in immigration policies, or would move overseas. The result was an increased net number of human capital flows thanks to the exclusive channels of migration and mobility put in place by governments willing to harness talent:

This takes place in the context of two fundamental and interrelated processes: the development of internal labour markets by employers, on the one hand, and of the institutional framework by governments to facilitate the global interchange of skills, on the other. The principal flows of highly skilled workers today reflect the global expansion of world trade, the international expansion of trans-national corporations, and the activities of institutions such as governments and recruitment agencies. (Salt 1997, p. 3)

Salt put the institutional framework at the center of his analysis, foregoing the traditional databases of tertiary educated migrants. The questions about why and how these skills flow across border thus became a central point of scholarly interest for over a decade. However, the very concept of skills has, since then, become quite contentious. As tertiary education ceased being the primary marker of the highly skilled in immigration policies, the question arose of what type of skills make somebody a highly skilled person. Even today, the working definition changes from country to country, and depends, as we already noted, on the needs of the labour market, whether annually adjusted or not. Who can access the labour market depends to a great extent on the system of recognition of qualifications. This system differs from country to country (even within the European Union) and formal skills are defined through that system. Robyn Iredale clearly addressed the issue of the variety of definitions of "skill" in his work on five Western democracies (2001). He reviewed concepts of skills embedded in skilled immigration policies as regards health professionals. He showed that there are a plurality of concepts and approaches to the definition of "skills" within political and policy debates in these countries. His most important contribution is, however, the critical reading of theoretical approaches to the question of highly skilled immigration. He argues in particular that existing policies and approaches to definitions are prone to gender and racial bias. This bias is linked to the public preference for a certain type of migrant, who is viewed as unproblematic. According to Iredale, the biased conceptualisation of the highly skilled worker as a wanted and unproblematic migrant permeates policy discourses and blurs the definitions: there are indeed certain racial and gendered hierarchies in the migrant continuum (Iredale 2001). Similar concerns were voiced more recently by Boucher. In her 2019 article, she reviews concepts of "skill," which drives skilled immigration policies in five Western liberal democracies. The author brings to the fore the plurality of approaches and definitions of skill in political discourses. While indicating the danger of simplification and essentialisation, she argues that "greater attention by policy-makers and scholars of skilled immigration to the theoretical assumptions underpinning their preferred models of skilled immigration would better reveal the gendered and racialised biases of existing approaches to skills definition" (2019, p. 1). A critique of the notion of "skills" in the context of international migration has also been delivered by Williams (2007), who argued that skills are actually defined differently by various actors involved in highly skilled migration; the state, the city and the company (A. M. Williams 2007). This multilevel approach to skill definition further problematises the assumed straightforwardness of the concept.

For some authors, skills seem to be defined better in the context of global labour markets. Where "internationally marketable" skills are concerned, national optics and politics give way to a broader view of human capital as a limited resource on the global scale. Therefore the needs and attractiveness of international labour markets set the boundaries for the conceptualisation of the highly skilled migrants. Solimano (2008) proposed a classification of skills according to the demand that exists for them on the international professional labor markets. The individuals in possession of these skills are the target of the global talent hunt, meaning that they have a high propensity to move and look for greener pastures. Thus, the policymakers and businesses who try to lure them globally do not necessarily see them as permanent immigrants, but rather as temporary residents (cf. Iredale 2002). These migrants fall into one of the following categories (adapted from Solimano 2008):

(a) People defined as directly productive talent, such as entrepreneurs, engineers, and technicians. They are engaged directly in activities that lead to the actual production of goods and services.
(b) People defined as academic (indirect) talent, i.e. scientists, researchers, research managers, and scholars. They work at universities, research centres, and think tanks and are devoted to the production and/or acquisition of scientific and scholarly knowledge that may be eventually translated into commercially valuable products and inputs.
(c) People defined as talent in social sectors. They include medical doctors, nurses and teachers. This talent is engaged directly in the provision of critical social services such as health or education.

Solimano's proposal largely reflects the current set up of national immigration programs geared towards highly skilled and skilled migrants. The sectoral-based definitions that consider the actual shortages and needs are dominant in Europe, but also in temporary migration programs all over the globe. Most importantly, they change with labour market needs and go through the economic cycles (Enríquez and Triandafyllidou 2016).

2.2.3 Migrant, Expatriate or Mobile Professional?

The idea of international labour markets resonates with the vision of the global labour market within which the highly skilled can move more freely than other (i.e. less skilled) migrants (Callister et al. 2006; Favell 2009; Geddes 2003). In principle, their flows are uninterrupted and facilitated, and this enhanced mobility is a key differentiating feature from all other migrants, including those who enter via the more traditional highly skilled migrant route. That particular feature of the "highly skilled" group was not lost on Salt (1997). In his attempt to provide a working definition of the highly skilled migrant for the sake of public policy design, he noted that "migrant" is indeed the most problematic part of "highly-skilled migrant." Salt argued that highly skilled migrants are not seen as migrants, but mobile people. He suggested that those with high levels of educational attainment or occupations – which make them more likely to turn to international labour markets – often are not captured in migration statistics. These statistics tend to focus either on visa categories or on counting permanent residents, and rarely look at short-term, circular movements. However, highly skilled migrants enter under other visa streams (e.g. business visitors or visitors *tout court*) and, because of their high degree of mobility, may often remain mobile, rather than settling.[1] Hence, there is a sizable group of mobile people who are not enumerated as migrants, and thus are not captured on the radar of either scholars or policy-makers. While migration is the term most often used to describe the international movement of South-North or South-South migrants, when it comes to the international movement of individuals from the Global North, the term "mobility" is often used as an alternative by authors. This distinction underscores the difference in perception of movement from the Global North and from the Global South. Indeed, it has been argued that highly-skilled migrants from countries which bestow more mobility opportunities on its citizens (e.g. some North-Western European countries) are not tied to their immigration decision and if they do not reach their goals overseas, they have the choice of returning or moving elsewhere (Weinar 2019). Such mobility patterns – back-and-forth movement, rather than one-way – are also more acceptable now than they were in the past, e.g. thanks to the increased acceptance of dual nationality and internationalization of skills (Harvey 2012). This experience is not, however, shared by South-North highly-skilled migrants, whose passports do not always give them the same access to mobility. Indeed, the patterns of South-North highly-skilled migrants remain more settlement-bound, which brings us back again to the distinction in integration between the highly-skilled migrants from the Global North and from the Global South. This clear distinction in patterns between what is called migration and what is called mobility has an important impact on conceptualisation of highly skilled migrants and the measurement of the same (Box 2.2).

---

[1] A migrant is normally defined as a person residing in a state other than their state of nationality or habitual residence for between 3 and 12 months, or more than 12 months, distinguishing between temporary and long-term migration. https://refugeesmigrants.un.org/definitions [accessed 25 October 2019] The UN Migration Agency (IOM) defines a migrant as any person who is moving or has moved across an international border or within a State away from his/her habitual place of residence, regardless of (1) the person's legal status; (2) whether the movement is voluntary or involuntary; (3) what the causes for the movement are; or (4) what the length of the stay is. https://www.un.org/en/sections/issues-depth/migration/index.html [accessed 25 October 2019].

Box 2.2: Highly Skilled Migrants as Mobile People

To support early policy development, Salt (1997) proposed a categorisation[2] of temporary highly skilled migrants based on occupation and mobility patterns. He aimed at a conceptualisation that would accommodate the diversity of the highly skilled, with the varied composition of the flows, and differing patterns of mobility. Most importantly, he excluded from his discussion permanent immigrants, business travellers, and those migrants who experience deskilling in their new occupations in the country of destination, working in "unskilled" or "lesser-skilled" professions, despite having tertiary education. In other words, he was interested in foreigners who are employed in occupations normally assigned to highly skilled (educated) people, but who do not migrate through the special immigration streams for highly skilled, but rather through various short-term mobility schemes. In this sense, he introduced a clear distinction between migrants using immigration channels and mobile professionals in the field of highly skilled migration studies.

In a similar vein, Mahroum (1999) proposed five distinct categories of people whom he classified as highly skilled migrants, but in his definition they were just mobile. He used NOC classification to define their level of skills and occupations, and gave them nicknames that reinforced the notion of temporariness, key to the definition of highly skilled migrant in his view. These were: (i) Managers & Executives, whom Mahroum nicknamed "accidental tourists", (ii) Engineers & Technicians – "economy class passengers", (iii) Academics & Scientists – "pilgrims", (iv) Entrepreneurs – "explorers", and (v) Students – "passengers".

The focus on temporariness and mobility as opposed to settlement and migration in early work on highly skilled migration reflected the then reality of Global North migrants pursuing career development in an international context. Indeed, most of the categories identified by these scholars were related to what has been called the global mobility of talent (Crowley-Henry and Al Ariss 2018; McNulty and Hutchings 2016). This term is widely used in business studies concerned with the mobility of these so-called organisational "expatriates," who are on specific packages and have usually been posted abroad by their companies. Debate around the mobility of this specific group of people seems to be present neither in policy nor in public debate. It even might be said to be an invisible migration stream. The main characteristic of this type of highly skilled migration is that it tends to be short-to-medium term, but there are some other features defining this group. Beaverstock (2016) undertakes conceptualisation of skilled international migration through the lens of international producer service firms. He narrows down his definition to those "highly skilled, professional and managerial, and knowledge-intensive human resources" (p. 1) who

---

[2] Salt called it a typology, but, arguably, he does not present "types" but "categories."

are deployed globally as a part of a company's organizational strategy. From the view of business studies, this global mobility of talent is a normalised practice in the training or managing strategies of multinational or international companies. Such mobility has become ubiquitous as companies organize their internal labor markets and client relationships more globally, introducing flexibility in the mobility of highly skilled staff. These changes prompt businesses to seek support from state policymakers for their new human resources management models. They lobby for more flexible talent mobility policies and tools (e.g. fast tracking, exemptions or special programs). Some use the existing legal frameworks to their advantage, as e.g. non-EU businesses employing workers with EU passports specifically to go for assignments in the European Union.[3]

Salt's categorisation included professionals who move for temporary stays abroad somewhat independently from the company (e.g. consultants). Business literature coined the term "self-initiated expatriate" to refer to this particular group of people (Cerdin and Selmer 2014; Doherty 2013; Fu et al. 2017; Froese and Peltokorpi 2013; Jokinen et al. 2008; Elo and Habti 2019), distinguishing them from the "organizational expatriates" mentioned above. The definition has not been clearly specified, however. Cerdin and Selmer offer a review of a variety of concepts and definitions present in this literature, and then propose a definition based on four conceptual, rather than quantitatively measurable, criteria to differentiate self-initiated expatriates from other migrants: (1) a self-initiated international relocation, (2) at least intentions of regular employment, (3) intentions of a temporary stay, and (4) skilled/professional qualifications (Cerdin and Selmer 2014). These criteria effectively remove any overlaps with traditional "organisational expatriate" or highly skilled immigrant who comes through permanent immigration channels.

Indeed, the criteria above are so broad that they capture the majority of highly skilled movers – many migrants move initially on temporary visas, including those on H1B visas to the US, which are renewable, and they include all highly skilled immigrants to EU member states, where all migrants have temporary status before obtaining permanent resident status. While many migrants do shift from temporary to long-term or permanent status, data are not available to indicate how widespread that shift is. Indeed, the lack of data more broadly for many of these sub-categories means that further study is often carried out as smaller qualitative studies, which contributes depth to the knowledge of particular groups, but does not necessarily contribute to the breadth of knowledge of the wide variation among highly skilled migrants. Also, the intention of a temporary stay and thus lack of integration is elusive, as we will discuss in more detail in Chap. 3. This is so not only because most temporary highly skilled migrants, even if they are considered to be exempt from integration requirements, do adjust to their local culture (van Bochove and Engbersen 2015), but because a common phenomenon among permanent migrants is the "myth of return", or "accidental migrant", i.e. they originally intended to emigrate

---

[3] Agnieszka Weinar interviews with Ubisoft and ABB employees, March 2017 and June 2017.

temporarily, but happen to stay (Safran 1991; Carling and Pettersen 2014; Dustmann 1999; Klekowski von Koppenfels 2014). Mobile professionals have similar challenges as other international migrants – learning a new language, finding suitable employment – but do not have the support of their company, as do organisational expatriates. It is thus, in our opinion, impossible to distinguish them from "migrants" (Al Ariss 2010), because they meet all definitions of international highly skilled migrants. We want to note that the term "expatriate" has become broadly – and erroneously – applied to all migrants from the Global North (Klekowski von Koppenfels 2014, see also Chap. 4). Understood through the discussion above, however, the "expatriate", whether organizational or self-initiated, may come from either the Global North or the Global South. Key is that the individual have the skills and/or training which qualify him/ her as a highly skilled migrant and immigration policies recognise them as such. Very often, however, highly skilled migrants do not get such recognition.

2.3   Contested Categories

In recent years, scholarship has started contesting the conventional definitions of highly skilled migrants. Many researchers have rightly noted that immigration policies targeting workers are missing out on many highly skilled migrants, who are not identified as such. In 2016, Canadian Immigration Minister John McCallum made headlines when he argued that "all immigrants are economic immigrants" regardless of whether they entered Canada as refugees, family unification migrants or labor migrants.[4] He underlined that all of them, regardless of their visa status upon entry, will contribute to the Canadian economy, and are, further, needed to develop that economy, so treating them differently according to immigration policy categorisation is essentially nonsensical. His comments are particularly illuminating when we reflect on the fact that 65% of permanent immigrants to Canada in any given year are assigned to the so-called economic stream – yet this figure includes both workers and members of their families, obscuring administrative data for this group (IRCC 2016).

The same can be said about the prevailing definitions and data sources on highly skilled migrants: more often than not, administrative data on migrants capture those who come explicitly as highly skilled migrants, through specific streams, but it does not capture any other immigrants: international students, who come as students, but who may be already highly skilled in some domains; highly skilled who may accept migrating as low-skilled workers; skilled refugees and spouses who enter as refugees or asylum-seekers, spouses or intended spouses. We briefly discuss these groups, with reference to inclusion in the highly skilled.

---

[4] https://globalnews.ca/video/2579468/immigration-minister-calls-all-newcomers-economic-immigrants [accessed 29 March 2019].

2.3.1 International Students

OECD in its publication on highly skilled migration included a chapter on international students (Tremblay 2002). In 2002, this approach – including international students as highly skilled migrants - was a fairly common, intuitive approach. International students, defined as individuals who were in education beyond 15 years of age and who crossed international borders to enrol, became one of the targets of policies attracting skilled workers. However, they are not, as a group, strictly speaking, highly skilled migrants, whether measured by the criterion of educational attainment (tertiary degree achieved), the criterion of professional experience, or even of salary. Rather, their inclusion in the category of highly skilled migrant reflected the possibility of their retention in the country of destination after graduation, as a highly skilled immigrant, promoted *inter alia* by the International Labour Organisation (Kuptsch 2006).

The prevailing idea was thus that international students are per definition skilled because they have the potential to become highly skilled down the road. If they pay for their education and then stay to work in highly skilled occupations in the country of destination, this certainly does seem to be a win-win situation for both migrants and for the country of destination. Hence, policy makers have been eager to portray students as potentially highly skilled migrants, or at least: wanted migrants, those who will be easily adaptable to the domestic labour market and society (Hawthorne 2008, 2010). Indeed, many authors have demonstrated that the experience of being an international student increases the likelihood of becoming a skilled migrant after graduation (F. L. N. Li et al. 1996; Salt 1997; Koser and Salt 1997; Cairns 2017). Moreover, some scholars have claimed that the networks developed by international students also serve to increase highly skilled immigration, because they support their colleagues and friends from the country of origin in their emigration project. The circulation of skilled labour is thus partly due to the presence of international students (Khadria 2001; Koser and Salt 1997; Gribble 2008; Vertovec 2002) (Khadria 2001; Vertovec 2002; Gribble 2008).

However, in the light of the knowledge accumulated over the last 15 years, it has become clear that the status of permanent highly skilled worker is not an obvious outcome for international students. Already in 1999 Mahroum classified students as passengers rather than stayers, people who stay but also return, or move forward (Mahroum 1999). As to skills, several researchers have raised some doubts as to how to address the educational attainment in students. For example, Skeldon (2018) questions that all students should be considered as highly skilled. He brings to light the variability of skill levels attainable through formal tertiary education (e.g. a range from BA to PhD), type of skills (e.g. technical or not), and fields of studies (e.g. humanities or medicine). These differences are important, and they showcase the point made by Williams (2007) about the invisible yet real, unspoken yet solid skill hierarchy, which changes from actor to actor and is socially constructed.

The character of skills is not the only headache. Some authors noted that it is very difficult to actually collect data on international students as highly skilled immigrants: to establish the boundaries of the group, there should be a clear distinction between those in the process of training and those already trained, those who work during their studies, and those who wait until graduation (Skeldon 2018; She and Wotherspoon 2013). So when does the international student stop being a student and becomes a highly skilled migrant? Or otherwise: when does the student cease to be a student? From the administrative perspective, we are talking about the change in status (from student visa to permanent residency, or to a work permit for example). But it is not sure that a student will get a shot at the highly skilled position, so it may be that they undergo deskilling to stay.

This conceptual conundrum has been addressed in recent work of Raghuram, who argued that student migration is a key component of knowledge migration (Raghuram 2013). The term "knowledge migrant" has been used the most in the field of human resource management studies and education studies to denote highly skilled migrants (A. Williams and Baláž 2014). In this sense, the "knowledge" is not really defined in standardised terms, it is defined by the participants in the field it is applied in. In business studies, these are people who have the knowledge that is needed in the given sector. Scientists, researchers and students make part of this category, although they are not necessarily workers (Ackers 2005). In the 2013 article, Raghuram shows that the term "knowledge migrant" becomes more and more blurred as knowledge becomes central to any migration project. This is migrant selectivity at play: migrants without knowledge run higher risks and costs of migration. In this context refugees, economic and family migrants tend to engage in knowledge acquisition, at all stages of migration. This generalised run towards knowledge blurs the distinction between international students and other categories of migrants, and in our opinion also blurs the categories within the highly skilled field. Raghuram postulates that international students are still the "quintessential knowledge-seeking migrants" (p. 149) and that their distinctiveness can be deduced from their primary motive to move: studying.

The concept of "knowledge migrant" contests immigration policy-centered definition, driven by a variety of visas and permits, where the main motive to migrate defines the migrant. It can be neat for policy makers, but leaves us with a conceptual Gordian knot. The ambiguity of classification of international students has meant that they have become a subject to a separate research field, which offers more contextual definitions, depending on the actual case study that is presented (King and Raghuram 2013; Cairns 2014; De Wit et al. 2008).

2.3.2   Spouses – Trailing or Not

"Trailing spouse" has been a dominant label attached to a skilled spouse of an international professional for three decades now. It was first used by scholars in business studies, who examined the obstacles to international mobility among managers. The biggest obstacle that they identified was so-called "dual career couple," in which the spouse was reluctant to give up her career (L. L. Jean-Yves 1987; Eby 2001; Harvey

1998). Michael Harvey, who established the category of "trailing spouse" defined them as skilled individuals, mostly women, who followed their husbands and had to renounce their careers for the time of the move (Harvey 1998; van Bochove and Engbersen 2015). In these works, the "classic" travelling or trailing spouses have been firmly categorised as high-income expatriates who move in the bubble of intra-corporate transfers. Migration of this group has not been thus of major interest to any of the migration scholars for a long time. It wasn't until gender dimension of highly skilled migration entered under the radar of migration scholars very recently (Triandafyllidou and Isaakyan 2016; Kofman 2000) that researchers have started turning our attention to the plethora of nuances of spousal migration, especially among the highly skilled.

First, it has been acknowledged that most of the highly skilled spouses in dual career couples are not "classic" trailing spouses, but spouses accompanying a regular highly skilled migrant (i.e. not an intra-corporate transferee) to the new county of destination (Raghuram 2004; Purkayastha 2005; Vergés Bosch and González Ramos 2013, Cooke 2001; Pixley 2008; Eby 2001; Mäkelä, Känsälä, and Suutari 2011; van der Klis and Mulder 2008). This might be as well a new phenomenon, which was not so widespread – or perhaps not so well-known – a couple of decades ago. The global shift to immigration policies that favour skilled immigrants have had a rather unintended consequence: an influx of spouses. Whereas the classic "organisational expatriate" was the purely temporary migrant and the spouse was indeed a "trailing spouse," often without the right to work, highly skilled immigrants nowadays can settle in countries that pursue skilled settlement migration programs that can cater also to the spouse. So there is less "trailing" and more "family reunification" all around the globe.

Second, the travelling spouse is not necessarily a woman. There is a breadth of literature on gendered migration that focuses on women' experience, but men are more and more represented among migrants' spouses (Amcoff and Niedomysl 2015), whether in heterosexual or homosexual partnerships (McPhail et al. 2016). This is rather uncharted waters, as the work on highly skilled professional women has only just started and we do not know enough about their family dynamics (Kõu and Bailey 2017; Gropas and Bartolini 2016). This gender aspect further complicates the definition of highly skilled migrant.

Third, spouses of highly skilled migrants tend to be highly skilled themselves (Cangià 2018; Raghuram 2004); it is a general truth in social studies that individuals often choose partners with similar educational levels and social backgrounds. The policy focus on highly skilled migrant workers in countries like Canada or Australia brought a wave of skilled spouses, who are, however not defined as highly skilled migrants themselves. Although entering under the economic migrant umbrella, they are registered statistically as dependents of highly skilled migrants (IRCC 2016). This methodology skews the data and requires additional data processing e.g. to see educational levels of spouses, which is gathered in some countries (e.g. Canada and Australia), but by no means all.

Fourth, because they are generally overlooked in immigration policies, and may not have the right to work in formal employment, they often suffer acute deskilling or job-loss in the migration process (Purkayastha 2005; Kranz 2019; Isaakyan and Triandafyllidou 2018).[5] They might be the top example of why skills and occupation do not help to define who a highly skilled migrant is, as they end up either unemployed for long periods, or chronically underemployed.

All in all, scholars generally have not yet considered spouses of highly skilled migrants as highly skilled migrants in their own right (e.g. Reslow 2018). This might be again dictated by the policy reality, where the motive for migration (in this case: following a spouse) is dominant for any definition. However, since the policy makers like Minister McCallum have started to appreciate the characteristics of this stream of spouses, there has been increased interest. The work taking this perspective is scarce and developing, with the possible inclusion of this category in the definition of highly skilled to come.

2.3.3   Refugees – Reluctant Non-workers

Are refugees highly skilled migrants? Overall, the answer used to be a "no." Educational attainment or professional experience of refugees have not been of much consequence. In countries with permanent immigration programs (most prominently the US, Canada and Australia), refugees have been conceptualised as part of a strategy fulfilling humanitarian goals, rather than seeing refugees as potential net positive economic contributors to the economy. Nonetheless, they are granted the right to work upon arrival, with refugee status recognised (Knowles 2016; Colic-Peisker and Tilbury 2006).

In the European Union, which does not have the same refugee resettlement programs as Canada, the United States and Australia, the discussion is focused instead on asylum seekers, i.e. migrants who apply for refugee status on EU territory. As they are seen, on the one hand, as humanitarian cases and, on the other, as having a pending status and, above all, not seen as economic migrants in the sense of having an expected overall contribution to the economy, they are often not entitled to work (there is some variation across the EU; Hatton 2016) until their status as refugees has been recognized, a process which may take months, sometimes years (Berthoud 2000; Bloch and Schuster 2002, Hatton 2016). In addition, they are often disparaged as so-called "bogus asylum seekers", said to have no credible claim to refugee status, and to be trying to benefit from the European welfare state (Hatton 2016; Huysmans 2006).

Once they have had refugee status recognized and they are entitled to work, refugees nonetheless face a range of barriers to employment, although there has been progress in recent years. Even so, for refugees who arrive in the country of destination without formal proof of their academic and professional qualifications or work

---

[5] See e.g. the survey of Internations, a global group for expats, mobile professionals and other skilled migrants. https://www.internations.org/expat-insider/2015/expat-spouses [accessed 29 March 2019].

experience, as many do (Phillimore and Goodson 2016), it is difficult to demonstrate education or skill level. Hence, refugees are more often than not automatically treated as low-skilled workers (Dustmann et al. 2016; Lergetporer et al. 2018) or may be confined to the secondary labour market, based on racial or ethnic bias (Colic-Peisker and Tilbury 2006). Those who prepared their move more meticulously and were able to bring evidence of qualifications or experience, could hope for local recognition and in the long run: the label of a highly skilled migrant. Many UN-led and EU-wide policy initiatives try to rectify the situation, especially since 2014.[6] Even so, Eggenhofer and colleagues, using a Bourdieusian notion of capital,[7] showed that the human and social capital of Afghani and Syrian refugees was strongly devalued, that attempts to employ their cultural capital encountered unfamiliar labor market rules, occupational identity threats, and status loss, and that acquisition and conversion of new capital is a complex and lengthy process (Eggenhofer-Rehart et al. 2018).

A more nuanced perspective on refugees and skills has been emerging in the aftermath of the so-called refugee crisis in Europe. There has been a clear change of the dominant discourse, with information on the declared skills of refugees now collected. Indeed, many Syrian refugees to Europe to 2018 had achieved tertiary education (Desiderio 2016; Eggenhofer-Rehart et al. 2018; Juran and Broer 2017). There has also been a big push to create opportunities for those refugees who fled the war during their studies, such as the gradual establishment of permanent and large-scale programs for university-aged youth (Streitwieser and Idriss 2017). Such approaches put refugees in the category of international students, and thus potentially highly skilled immigrants.

In refugee resettlement countries like Canada, where the understanding that "all migrants are economic migrants" has, as noted above, only just started to shine through, there is as yet only a nascent interest in the skills refugees can bring. Refugees may well be highly skilled migrants, as demonstrated by the experience of the Green card (highly skilled worker program) in Germany, which had a high number of refugees and displaced persons among its applicants (Pethe 2007). How these discoveries and assertions from the research community will change the definition of the highly skilled migrant (and thus affect the administrative data collections) is still the question of the future.

---

[6] http://www.aca-secretariat.be/index.php?id=1104 [accessed 21 January 2019].

https://www.mariecuriealumni.eu/news/science4refugees-initiative   [accessed   21 January 2019].

http://www.akademikmiras.org/en/yok-ve-multeciler [accessed 21 January 2019].

https://www.al-fanarmedia.org/2019/01/report-examines-progress-in-recognizing-refugees-credentials/ [accessed 21 January 2019].

https://www.unhcr.org/5bc07ca94.pdf [accessed 21 January 2019].

https://www.unhcr.org/ [accessed 21 January 2019].

[7] See Box 3.2.

2.4   Geography and Skills

In the last section of this chapter, we want to touch upon a notion of geography in definitions of the highly skilled migrants. This is the distinction between the highly skilled from the Global South – universally referred to as "migrants" – and the highly skilled from the Global North – nearly universally referred to as "expatriates" (Klekowski von Koppenfels 2014, 2015). This geographical distinction – accompanied by implicit, if not explicit, racial and ethnic bias, has an impact upon how the highly skilled are portrayed and defined; we will develop these ideas further in the subsequent chapters. In 1988, Gould developed a typology of the movements of highly skilled international migrants in Africa associated with levels of economic development of the countries of origin and destination. At that time, skilled migrants from Western developed countries – the Global North – were associated predominantly with a migrant that reflected the "organisational expatriate", or, in a sub-Saharan African context, often the humanitarian worker, while skilled migrants from developing countries – the Global South – were seen as permanent emigrants to the more developed world (Gould 1988). That typology was focused not on migration, but rather on development policy, examining concepts such as "brain drain," or the negative impact of emigration on development.

Within migration studies, more emphasis has been placed upon South-North migration, rather than on South-South or North-North. This emphasis emerges from the work done in the 1960s and 1970s by development economists who were interested in the effects of the movement of human capital from developing to developed countries (A. B. Zahlan ed. 1982; Adams Jr. 2003; Zhao et al. 2000; Koser and Salt 1997).

Moreover, migration from the Global South to Global North has been a dynamic force with a significant impact on the societies of the strongly developed OECD states. The research on the impact of highly skilled migration from the South on the country of origin – largely through a study of brain drain – has been thus complemented, and in many cases, substituted, by research on the impacts on the country of destination, including impact on native workers (Borjas 2005; Friedberg and Hunt 1995; Biavaschi et al. 2018) (Box 2.3).

Box 2.3: What Is the Impact of the Temporary Foreign Workers?
The Canadian TWF program, in place since 1973, was opened to all occupations in 2002. Instantly, the number of foreign workers has risen by 234.5% in the first decade (2002–2012). The largest increase has been in Western Canada (371.3%) and the lowest in Ontario (137.6%). As noted by Dominique Gross (2017), that increase took place regardless of the rising unemployment, especially during the financial crisis years, pointing to the adverse effects the programme had on domestic workers. Over her many publications, Gross has shown however, that the highly skilled temporary workers have less impact on the domestic workforce than low skilled ones. Gross has noted also the important policy considerations that must be taken under account regardless of the skill level of the TFW namely the need to incentivize the employers to invest in training of youth for occupations and in technological innovations.

Within studies on South-North migration, disproportionate interest has been paid to highly skilled migration from India and China. By far, these two countries of origin are the most represented among the recent articles in the leading population and geography journals.[8] This is not surprising, as India and China are now leading countries of origin for skilled migration and student migration to the US, Canada, Australia, and New Zealand, while ranking near the top also in the UK. They have the biggest populations and the growing culture of internationalisation of human capital (Lakha 1992; Kumar 2013; Gao et al. 2013; Sanfilippo and Weinar 2017). These two groups dominate research that asks questions from the perspective of the countries of destination, but also from the perspective of individual migrants: integration in host society, labour market success, skill development and career prospects, return and transnational business networks (Czaika and Toma 2017; Fernando and Cohen 2016; Kirk et al. 2017; Siddiqui and Tejada 2014; W. Li and Lo 2012; Yao 2012).

In contrast, the studies on highly skilled migration from Sub-Saharan Africa still focus predominantly on the impacts on the country of origin, hence they develop further the development perspective (Clemens and Pettersson 2008; Capps et al. 2012; Creese and Wiebe 2012). There is rarely a question on how highly skilled African migrants develop their country of destination or how they contribute with their knowledge to the global economy. The various treatment reserved for various geographies reflects a certain hierarchy of issues that can be tackled in relation to their highly skilled migrants. In this view, the political and racial bias is perpetuated and the highly skilled label has different connotations.

North-North migration of the highly skilled is another widely researched topic. Yet, as noted earlier, it is usually not called migration, but mobility. There are four geography-related aspects to this field of research. First, intra-EU mobility, a prime example of North-North migration, is a type of mobility confined to a geo-political space. In this space, 40% of movers have tertiary education, so they can be regarded as North-North highly skilled migrants (Gropas and Bartolini 2016). The EU case is a specific case, where the data on intra-EU mobility is not easy to get, because these highly skilled workers are not captured through any dedicated immigration programme. Second, contemporary North-North migration is often portrayed as quantitatively inconsequential (Weinar 2018), as well as having no integration or political ramifications, and thus not interesting to study. Third, contemporary North-North migration is erroneously not seen as permanent migration, so the mobility of highly skilled (including students) in this geographical space is perceived as temporary and circular at best (Klekowski von Koppenfels 2014). Fourth, there is little conceptual clarity about who the "North-North migrant" is. The perception that all North-North migrants are highly skilled seems to permeate the field (even, to some extent, as regards intra-EU mobility). In addition, concepts such as "life-style migration" (King et al. 2000; Benson and O'reilly 2009) and "love migration" (D'Aoust 2013; Sinke 1999) are conflated with highly skilled migration and in result, the

---

[8] Agnieszka Weinar e-journal database content review, 10–15 January 2019.

predominant idea is that North-North migration is not only unproblematic, it is also a personal happiness pursuit by highly skilled migrants who enjoy the benefit of choice. There has been enough research on North-North migration to suggest that these assumptions are incorrect, but not enough to give a complete picture of these migration flows. We will address those in more detail in Chap. 4.

To complicate the issues, within business management literature, North-North and North-South migration is often conflated. The studies of "organisational expatriate" mobility are nearly exclusively about mobility from Western developed countries. Their destination can be to other developed countries or to the countries in the Global South (Beaverstock 2017, 1996). The added complexity of today's global mobility of professionals and their international career development changes the old patterns (Meyskens et al. 2009). Many Western international highly skilled movers can be classified as "self-initiated expatriate" (Cerdin and Selmer 2014). Some of these emerging populations of expatriates have been termed "international itinerants" (Banai and Harry 2004) or "independent internationally mobile professionals" (McKenna and Richardson 2007). Interestingly enough, the term "migrant" is still avoided, as it is in all other cases of North-North migration. This labelling approach, coupled with the highly skilled migrations streams open for South migrants contributes to racialisation of the concept of the highly skilled migrant.

Finally, the understudied geographical mobility, South-South migration of highly skilled is in its nascent state (Ratha and Shaw 2007; Botha and Rasool 2011; Facchini et al. 2011). With the emergence of Africa as a business hub, this mobility will become a more important focus of research. For the moment, however, it is largely ignored, leaving the overall impression that South-North is the defining line of the geographies of highly skilled migration.

2.5   Conclusions

As we have shown in this Chapter, the definitions of the highly skilled vary. They have been mainly driven by the administrative data used to meet policy needs. The research in this area has been very much policy oriented and until recently has developed in two main fields of study: public policy and management studies. However, with the evolution of the research field, the definitions have been nuanced by the contributions from other scholars: sociologists, anthropologists, and those in the field of education. Current debates on how to define a highly skilled migrant evolve nowadays around the concept of skill measurement, employability and educational attainment. What seems to emerge from these debates is a consensus that the definition of the highly skilled is very context-dependent and can be adapted to particular needs. It is thus still more utilitarian than academic. Policy needs seem to be crucial in this case, more than in any other migration category.

In the next Chapter we will delve deeper into the lived experience of the highly skilled to determine the impact of the policies that define them. We will particularly look at their integration, keeping in mind all the different moving parts of their definition.

References

Ackers, L. (2005). Moving people and knowledge: Scientific mobility in the European union1. *International Migration, 43*(5), 99–131.

Adams Jr, R. H. (2003). *International migration, remittances, and the brain drain: A study of 24 labor-exporting countries.*World Bank Policy Research Working Paper, Washington.

Al Ariss, A. (2010). Modes of engagement: Migration, self-initiated expatriation, and career development. *Career Development International, 15*(4), 338–358.

Amcoff, J., & Niedomysl, T. (2015). Is the tied returnee male or female? The trailing spouse thesis reconsidered. *Population, Space and Place, 21*(8), 872–881.

Banai, M., & Harry, W. (2004). Boundaryless global careers: The international itinerants. *International Studies of Management & Organization, 34*(3), 96–120.

Beach, C. M., Green, A. G., & Worswick, C. (2007). Impacts of the point system and immigration policy levers on skill characteristics of Canadian immigrants. In *Immigration* (pp. 349–401). Emerald Group Publishing Limited.

Beaverstock, J. V. (1996). Migration, knowledge and social interaction: Expatriate labour within investment banks. *Area, 28*(4), 459–470.

Beaverstock, J. V. (2005). Transnational elites in the city: British highly-skilled inter-company transferees in Yew York city's financial district. *Journal of Ethnic and Migration Studies, 31*(2), 245–268.

Beaverstock, J. V. (2016). Migration: Skilled international labor. In *International encyclopedia of geography: People, the earth, environment and technology: People, the earth, environment and technology* (pp. 1–12).

Beaverstock, J. V. (2017). Migration: Skilled international labor. In *International encyclopedia of geography* (pp. 1–12). American Cancer Society.

Becker, G. S. (1975, 1930). *Human capital.* Vol. 5. Human Behavior and Social Institutions; 5. National Bureau of Economic Research: distributed by Columbia University Press.

Beine, M., Docquier, F., & Rapoport, H. (2007). Measuring international skilled migration: A new database controlling for age of entry. *The World Bank Economic Review, 21*(2), 249–254.

Beine, M., Docquier, F., & Rapoport, H. (2008). Brain drain and human capital formation in developing countries: Winners and losers. *The Economic Journal, 118*(528), 631–652.

Benson, M., & O'reilly, K. (2009). Migration and the search for a better way of life: A critical exploration of lifestyle migration. *The Sociological Review, 57*(4), 608–625.

Berthoud, R. (2000). Ethnic employment penalties in Britain. *Journal of Ethnic and Migration Studies, 26*(3), 389–416.

Bhargava, A., Docquier, F., & Moullan, Y. (2011). Modeling the effects of physician emigration on human development. *Economics & Human Biology, 9*(2), 172–183.

Biavaschi, C., Burzyński, M., Elsner, B., & Machado, J. (2018). Taking the skill Bias out of global migration. *Journal of Development Economics, 142*, 102317.

Bielewska, A. (2018). Game of labels: Identification of highly skilled migrants. *Identities, 20180919*, 1–19.

Bloch, A., & Schuster, L. (2002). Asylum and welfare: Contemporary debates. *Critical Social Policy, 22*(3), 393–414.

Borjas, G. J. (1987). Immigrants, minorities, and labor market competition. *ILR Review, 40*(3), 382–392.

Borjas, G. J. (2005). The labor-market impact of high-skill immigration. *American Economic Review, 95*(2), 56–60.

Botha, C. J., & Rasool, F. (2011). The nature, extent and effect of skills shortages on skills migration in South Africa. *SA Journal of Human Resource Management, 9*(1), 1–12.

Boucher, A. K. (2019). How 'skill' definition affects the diversity of skilled immigration policies. *Journal of Ethnic and Migration Studies, 0*(0), 1–18.

Bouvier, L. F., & Simcox, D. (1995). Foreign-born professionals in the United States. *Population and Environment, 16*(5), 429–444.

Brettell, C. B., & Hollifield, J. F. (2014). *Migration theory: Talking across disciplines*. New York: Routledge.

Cairns, D. (2014). *Youth transitions, international student mobility and spatial reflexivity: Being mobile? London*. New York: Palgrave Macmillan.

Cairns, D. (2017). Exploring student mobility and graduate migration: Undergraduate mobility propensities in two economic crisis contexts. *Social & Cultural Geography, 18*(3), 336–353.

Callister, P., Bedford, R., Didham, R. A., & Statistics New Zealand. (2006). *Globalisation, gendered migration and labour markets*. Department of Labour.

Cangià, F. (2018). Precarity, imagination, and the mobile life of the 'Trailing Spouse'. *Ethos, 46*(1), 8–26.

Capps, R., McCabe, K., & Fix, M. (2012). *Diverse streams: African migration to the United States*. Washington: Migration Policy Institute.

Carling, J., & Pettersen, S. V. (2014). Return migration intentions in the integration – Transnationalism matrix. *International Migration, 52*(6), 13–30.

Carrington, M. W., & Detragiache, M. E. (1998). *How big is the brain drain?* (pp. 98–102). Washington: International Monetary Fund.

Cerdin, J.-L., & Selmer, J. (2014). Who is a self-initiated expatriate? Towards conceptual clarity of a common notion. *The International Journal of Human Resource Management, 25*(9), 1281–1301.

Cerna, L. (2013). Understanding the diversity of EU migration policy in practice: The implementation of the blue card initiative. *Policy Studies, 34*(2), 180–200.

Checkel, J. T. (1997). International norms and domestic politics: Bridging the rationalist—constructivist divide. *European Journal of International Relations, 3*(4), 473–495.

Clemens, M. A., & Pettersson, G. (2008). New data on African health professionals abroad. *Human Resources for Health, 6*(1), 1.

Colic-Peisker, V., & Tilbury, F. (2006). Employment niches for recent refugees: Segmented labour market in twenty-first century Australia. *Journal of Refugee Studies, 19*(2), 203–229.

Cooke, T. J. (2001). 'Trailing Wife'or 'trailing mother'? The effect of parental status on the relationship between family migration and the labor-market participation of married women. *Environment and Planning A, 33*(3), 419–430.

Creese, G., & Wiebe, B. (2012). 'Survival employment': Gender and deskilling among African immigrants in Canada. *International Migration, 50*(5), 56–76.

Crowley-Henry, M., & Al Ariss, A. (2018). Talent management of skilled migrants: Propositions and an agenda for future research. *The International Journal of Human Resource Management, 29*(13), 2054–2079. https://doi.org/10.1080/09585192.2016.1262889.

Cunha, F., & Heckman, J. (2007). The technology of skill formation. *The American Economic Review, 97*(2), 31–47.

Czaika, M., & Parsons, C. R. (2017). The gravity of high-skilled migration policies. *Demography, 54*(2), 603–630.

Czaika, M., & Toma, S. (2017). International academic mobility across space and time: The case of Indian academics. *Population, Space and Place, 23*(8), e2069.

D'Aoust, A.-M. (2013). In the name of love: Marriage migration, governmentality, and technologies of love. *International Political Sociology, 7*(3), 258–274.

de Haas, H., Natter, K., & Vezzoli, S. (2018). Growing restrictiveness or changing selection? The nature and evolution of migration policies. *International Migration Review, 52*(2), 324–367. August, imre.12288.

De Wit, H., Agarwal, P., Said, M. E., Sehoole, M. T., & Sirozi, M. (2008). *The dynamics of international student circulation in a global context*. Rotterdam: Sense Publishers Rotterdam.

Desiderio, M. V. (2016). *Integrating refugees into host country labor markets: Challenges and policy options*. Washington: Migration Policy Institute.

Docquier, F., & Marfouk, A. (2006). International migration by education attainment, 1990–2000. In *International migration, remittances and the brain drain* (pp. 151–199). Washington: World Bank.

Docquier, F., & Rapoport, H. (2012). Globalization, brain drain, and development. *Journal of Economic Literature, 50*(3), 681–730.

Docquier, F., Lindsay Lowell, B., & Marfouk, A. (2009). A gendered assessment of highly skilled emigration. *Population and Development Review, 35*(2), 297–321.

Doherty, N. (2013). Understanding the self-initiated expatriate: A review and directions for future research. *International Journal of Management Reviews, 15*(4), 447–469.

Dumont, J.-C., & Lemaître, G. (2005). *Counting immigrants and expatriates in OECD countries.* Paris: OECD Publishing.

Dustmann, C. (1999). Temporary migration, human capital, and language fluency of migrants. *Scandinavian Journal of Economics, 101*(2), 297–314.

Dustmann, C., Fasani, F., Frattini, T., Minale, L., & Schönberg, U. (2016). *On the economics and politics of refugee migration.* Munich: Center for Economic Studies and Ifo Institute. https:// papers.ssrn.com/sol3/papers.cfm?abstract_id=2850399

Dzvimbo, K. P. (2003). The international migration of skilled human capital from developing countries. In *A case study prepared for a regional training conference on improving tertiary education in sub-Saharan Africa* (pp. 23–25). Things That Work.

Eby, L. T. (2001). The Boundaryless career experiences of mobile spouses in dual-earner marriages. *Group & Organization Management, 26*(3), 343–368.

Eggenhofer-Rehart, P. M., Latzke, M., Pernkopf, K., Zellhofer, D., Mayrhofer, W., & Steyrer, J. (2018). Refugees' career capital welcome? Afghan and Syrian Refugee job seekers in Austria. *Journal of Vocational Behavior*, Vocational Behavior of Refugees: How Do Refugees Seek Employment, Overcome Work-related Challenges, and Navigate Their Careers?, *105*(April), 31–45.

Elo, M., & Habti, D. (2019). Self-initiated expatriation rebooted: A puzzling reality–a challenge to migration research and its future direction. In *In global mobility of highly skilled people* (pp. 293–304). Springer.

Enríquez, C. G., & Triandafyllidou, A. (2016). Female high-skilled emigration from Southern Europe and Ireland after the crisis. In A. Triandafyllidou & I. Isaakyan (Eds.), *High-skill migration and recession: gendered perspectives* (pp. 44–68). Migration: Diasporas and Citizenship. London: Palgrave Macmillan UK.

Espenshade, T. J., Usdansky, M. L., & Chung, C. Y. (2001). Employment and earnings of foreign-born scientists and engineers. *Population Research and Policy Review, 20*(1), 81–105.

Facchini, G., Mayda, A. M., & Mendola, M. (2011). *South-South migration and the labor market: Evidence from South Africa.* Washington: World Bank.

Favell, A. (2009). Immigration, migration and free movement in the making of Europe. In *European identity* (pp. 167–189). Cambridge: Cambridge University Press.

Fernando, W. D. A., & Cohen, L. (2016). Exploring career advantages of highly skilled migrants: A study of Indian academics in the UK. *The International Journal of Human Resource Management, 27*(12), 1277–1298.

Franzoni, C., Scellato, G., & Stephan, P. (2012). Foreign-born scientists: Mobility patterns for 16 countries. *Nature Biotechnology, 30*(12), 1250–1253.

Friedberg, R. M., & Hunt, J. (1995). The impact of immigrants on host country wages, employment and growth. *Journal of Economic Perspectives, 9*(2), 23–44.

Froese, F. J., & Peltokorpi, V. (2013). Organizational expatriates and self-initiated expatriates: Differences in cross-cultural adjustment and job satisfaction. *The International Journal of Human Resource Management, 24*(10), 1953–1967.

Fu, C., Hsu, Y.-S., Shaffer, M. A., & Ren, H. (2017). A longitudinal investigation of self-initiated expatriate organizational socialization. *Personnel Review, 46*(2), 182–204.

Ganguli, I. (2014). Scientific brain drain and human capital formation after the end of the Soviet Union. *International Migration, 52*(5), 95–110.

Gao, L., Liu, X., & Zou, H. (2013). The role of human mobility in promoting Chinese outward FDI: A neglected factor? *International Business Review, 22*(2), 437–449.

Geddes, A. (2003). *The politics of migration and immigration in Europe.* London: Sage.

Gould, W. T. (1988). Skilled international labour migration. *Geoforum, 19*(4), 381–445.

Green, A. G., & Green, D. A. (1995). Canadian immigration policy: The effectiveness of the point system and other instruments. *Canadian Journal of Economics, 28*, 1006–1041.

Gribble, C. (2008). Policy options for managing international student migration: The sending country's perspective. *Journal of Higher Education Policy and Management, 30*(1), 25–39.

Gropas, R., & Bartolini, L. (2016). Southern European highly skilled female migrants in male-dominated sectors in times of crisis: A look into the IT and engineering sectors. In *High-skill migration and recession* (pp. 160–192). London: Springer.

Gross, D. M. (2017). Conditions for an efficient Canadian temporary foreign worker program: The case of Quebec. *Canadian Ethnic Studies, 49*(2), 99–119.

Harvey, M. (1998). Dual-career couples during international relocation: The trailing spouse. *The International Journal of Human Resource Management, 9*(2), 309–331.

Harvey, W. (2012). Brain circulation to the UK? Knowledge and investment flows from highly skilled British expatriates in Vancouver. *Journal of Management Development, 31*(2), 173–186.

Hatton, T. J. (2016). Refugees, asylum seekers, and policy in OECD countries. *American Economic Review, 106*(5), 441–445.

Hawthorne, L. (2008). The growing global demand for students as skilled migrants. In *Transatlantic council on migration's second plenary meeting,* New York.

Hawthorne, L. (2010). Demography, migration and demand for international students. In *Globalisation and tertiary education in the Asia-pacific: The changing nature of a dynamic market* (pp. 93–119). Singapore: World Scientific Publishing.

Huysmans, J. (2006). *The politics of insecurity: Fear, migration and asylum in the EU.* Routledge.

IRCC. (2016). *Facts and figures 2016.* http://www.cic.gc.ca/opendata-donneesouvertes/data/Facts_and_Figures_2016_PR_EN.pdf.

Iredale, R. (2001). The migration of professionals: Theories and typologies. *International Migration, 39*(5), 7–26.

Iredale, R., & Appleyard, R. (2001). *International migration of the highly skilled-introduction.* Geneva: IOM.

Isaakyan, I., & Triandafyllidou, A. (2018). Reflections on diaspora and soft power: Community building among female US expats in southern Europe. *Identities, 25*(6), 650–667.

Jean-Yves, L. L. (1987). Canadian managers' decision involving two-career couples. *Canadian Journal of Administrative Sciences / Revue Canadienne Des Sciences de l'Administration, 4*(2), 113–124.

Jokinen, T., Brewster, C., & Suutari, V. (2008). Career capital during international work experiences: Contrasting self-initiated expatriate experiences and assigned expatriation. *The International Journal of Human Resource Management, 19*(6), 979–998.

Joppke, C. (1999). *Immigration and the nation-state: The United States, Germany, and great Britain.* Oxford: Oxford University Press.

Juran, S., & Niclas Broer, P. (2017). A profile of Germany's refugee populations. *Population and Development Review, 43*(1), 149–157.

Kerr, S. P., Kerr, W., Ozden, & Parsons, C. (2016). *Global talent flows.* Washington: The World Bank.

Khadria, B. (2001). Shifting paradigms of globalization: The twenty-first century transition towards generics in skilled migration from India. *International Migration, 39*(5), 45–71.

King, R., & Raghuram, P. (2013). International student migration: Mapping the field and new research agendas. *Population, Space and Place, 19*(2), 127–137.

King, R., Warnes, A. M., Warnes, T., & Williams, A. M. (2000). *Sunset lives: British retirement migration to the Mediterranean.* Oxford: Berg.

Kirk, K., Bal, E., & Janssen, S. R. (2017). Migrants in liminal time and space: An exploration of the experiences of highly skilled Indian bachelors in Amsterdam. *Journal of Ethnic and Migration Studies, 43*(16), 2771–2787.

Klekowski von Koppenfels, A. (2014). *Migrants or expatriates?: Americans in Europe.* Springer.

Knowles, V. (2016). *Strangers at our gates: Canadian immigration and immigration policy, 1540–2015.* Dundurn.

Kofman, E. (2000). The invisibility of skilled female migrants and gender relations in studies of skilled migration in Europe. *International Journal of Population Geography, 6*(1), 45–59.

Koser, K., & Salt, J. (1997). The geography of highly skilled international migration. *Population, Space and Place, 3*(4), 285–303.

Kõu, A., & Bailey, A. (2017). 'Some people expect women should always be dependent': Indian Women's experiences as highly skilled migrants. *Geoforum, 85*, 178–186.

Kranz, D. (2019). The global North Goes to the global North minus? Intersections of the integration of highly skilled, non-Jewish female partner and spousal migrants from the global North in Israel. *International Migration, 57*, 192–207.

Krasner, S. D. (2009). *Power, the state, and sovereignty: Essays on international relations.* New York: Routledge.

Kumar, N. (2013). The importance of human capital in the early internationalisation of Indian knowledge-intensive service firms. *International Journal of Technological Learning, Innovation and Development 2, 6*(1–2), 21–41.

Kuptsch, C. (2006). Students and talent flow – The case of Europe: From castle to harbour. In *Competing for global talent* (pp. 33–61). Geneva: ILO.

Lakha, S. (1992). The internationalisation of Indian computer professionals. *South Asia: Journal of South Asian Studies, 15*(2), 93–113.

Lavenex, S. (1999). *The europeanisation of refugee policies: Between human rights and internal security.* http://cadmus.eui.eu/handle/1814/5314

Lergetporer, P., Piopiunik, M., & Simon, L. (2018). Do natives' beliefs about refugees' education level affect attitudes toward refugees? Evidence from a randomized survey experiments. In *SSRN scholarly paper ID 3129985*. Rochester: Social Science Research Network. https://papers.ssrn.com/abstract=3129985

Li, W., & Lo, L. (2012). New geographies of migration?: A Canada-US comparison of highly skilled Chinese and Indian migration. *Journal of Asian American Studies, 15*(1), 1–34.

Li, F. L. N., Findlay, A. M., Jowett, A. J., & Skeldon, R. (1996). Migrating to learn and learning to migrate: A study of the experiences and intentions of international student migrants. *International Journal of Population Geography, 2*(1), 51–67.

Libaers, D. (2014). Foreign-born academic scientists and their interactions with industry: Implications for university technology commercialization and corporate innovation management. *Journal of Product Innovation Management, 31*(2), 346–360.

Lowell, B. L. (2001). Skilled temporary and permanent immigrants in the United States. *Population Research and Policy Review, 20*(1–2), 33–58.

Lowell, B. L. (2005). *Policies and regulations for managing skilled international migration for work.* New York: United Nations, Mortality and Migration Section of the Population Division/DESA.

Mahroum, S. (1999). Highly skilled globetrotters: The international migration of human capital. In *Proceedings of the OECD workshop on science and technology labour markets, DSTI/STP/TIP (99)*, 2:168–185.

Mäkelä, L., Känsälä, M., & Suutari, V. (2011). The roles of expatriates' spouses among dual career couples. *Cross Cultural Management: An International Journal, 18*(2), 185–197.

McKenna, S., & Richardson, J. (2007). The increasing complexity of the internationally mobile professional: Issues for research and practice. *Cross Cultural Management: An International Journal, 14*(4), 307–320.

McLaughlan, G., & Salt, J. (2002). *Migration policies towards highly skilled foreign workers.* London: Home Office.

McNulty, Y., & Hutchings, K. (2016). Looking for global talent in all the right places: A critical literature review of non-traditional expatriates. *The International Journal of Human Resource Management, 27*(7), 699–728. https://doi.org/10.1080/09585192.2016.1148756.

McPhail, R., McNulty, Y., & Hutchings, K. (2016). Lesbian and gay expatriation: Opportunities, barriers and challenges for global mobility. *The International Journal of Human Resource Management, 27*(3), 382–406.

McSweeney, B. (1999). *Security, identity and interests: A sociology of international relations* (Vol. 69). Cambridge: Cambridge University Press.

Meyskens, M., Von Glinow, M. A., Werther, W. B., & Clarke, L. (2009). The paradox of international talent: Alternative forms of international assignments. *The International Journal of Human Resource Management, 20*(6), 1439–1450.

Naumann, E., Stoetzer, L. F., & Pietrantuono, G. (2018). Attitudes towards highly skilled and low-skilled immigration in Europe: A survey experiment in 15 European countries. *European Journal of Political Research, 57*(4), 1009–1030.

OECD. (1998). *SOPEMI 1997: Trends in international migration: Continuous annual report*. Paris: OECD.

Parsons, C. R., Rojon, S., Samanani, F., & Wettach, L. (2014). *Conceptualising international high-skilled migration*, no. 104: 26.

Peri, G., & Sparber, C. (2011). Highly educated immigrants and native occupational choice. *Industrial Relations: A Journal of Economy and Society, 50*(3), 385–411.

Pethe, H. (2007). Un-restricted agents? International migration of the highly skilled revisited. *Social Geography Discussions, 3*(2), 211–236.

Phillimore, J., & Goodson, L. (2016). Problem or opportunity? Asylum seekers, Refugees, employment and social exclusion in deprived Urban areas. *Urban Studies, 43*(10), 1715–1736. July.

Pixley, J. E. (2008). Life course patterns of career-prioritizing decisions and occupational attainment in dual-earner couples. *Work and Occupations, 35*(2), 127–163.

Purkayastha, B. (2005). Skilled migration and cumulative disadvantage: The case of highly qualified Asian Indian immigrant women in the US. *Geoforum, 36*(2), 181–196.

Raghuram, P. (2004). The difference that skills make: Gender, family migration strategies and regulated labour markets. *Journal of Ethnic and Migration Studies, 30*(2), 303–321.

Raghuram, P. (2013). Theorising the spaces of student migration. *Population, Space and Place, 19*(2), 138–154.

Rapoport, H., Lodigiani, E., Docquier, F., & Schiff, M. (2011). *Emigration and democracy*. Bonn: IZA. https://openknowledge.worldbank.org/handle/10986/3327

Ratha, D., & Shaw, W. (2007). *South-South migration and remittances* (p. 102). Washington: World Bank Publications.

Reslow, N. (2018). Unfulfilled expectations: The contradictions of Dutch policy on temporary migration. In *Characteristics of temporary migration in European-Asian transnational social spaces* (pp. 193–211). Springer.

Ruggles, Steven, J. Trent Alexander, Katie Genadek, Ronald Goeken, Matthew B. Schroeder, and Matthew Sobek. 2010. Integrated public use microdata series: Version 5.0 [Machine-Readable Database]. *Minneapolis: University of Minnesota* 42.

Safran, W. (1991). Diasporas in modern societies: Myths of homeland and return. *Diaspora: A Journal of Transnational Studies, 1*(1), 83–99.

Salt, J. (1997, January). *International movements of the highly skilled*. Paris: OECD Publishing.

Sanfilippo, M., & Weinar, A. (2017). *Chinese migration and economic relations with Europe*. London: Routledge.

She, Q., & Wotherspoon, T. (2013). International student mobility and highly skilled migration: A comparative study of Canada, the United States, and the United Kingdom. *Springerplus, 2*(1), 132.

Siddiqui, Z., & Tejada, G. (2014). *Development and highly skilled migrants: Perspectives from Indian diaspora and returnees, international development policy*. Article 4, Geneva: Graduate Institute of International and Development Studies .

Sinke, S. (1999). Migration for labor, migration for love: Marriage and family formation across Borders. *OAH Magazine of History, 14*(1), 17–21.

Skeldon, R. (2018). High-skilled migration and the limits of migration policies. In *High-Skilled Migration: Drivers and Policies* (pp. 48–64). Oxford: Oxford University Press. https://doi.org/10.1093/oso/9780198815273.003.0003.

Solimano, A. (2008). *The international mobility of talent*. New York: Oxford University Press.

Soysal, Y. N. (1994). *Limits of citizenship: Migrants and postnational membership in Europe*. Chicago: University of Chicago Press.

Streitwieser, B. & Cynthia Miller-Idriss. (2017). Higher education's response to the European refugee crisis: Challenges, strategies and opportunities. *The Globalization of Internationalization*. January 20, 2017.

Tremblay, K. (2002). Student mobility between and towards OECD countries: A comparative analysis. In *International mobility of the highly skilled* (pp. 39–67). Paris: OECD Publishing.

Triadafilopoulos, T. (2013). *Wanted and welcome?: Policies for highly skilled immigrants in comparative perspective.* New York: Springer Science & Business Media.

Triandafyllidou, A., & Isaakyan, I. (2014). *EU management of high skill migration.* Oxford: University of Oxford. http://cadmus.eui.eu//handle/1814/34706

Triandafyllidou, A., & Isaakyan, I. (eds). (2016). European policies to attract talent: The crisis and highly skilled migration policy changes. In *High-skill migration and recession. Migration, diasporas and citizenship.* London: Palgrave Macmillan.

van Bochove, M., & Engbersen, G. (2015). Beyond cosmopolitanism and expat bubbles: Challenging dominant representations of knowledge workers and trailing spouses. *Population Space and Place, 21*(4), 295–309.

van der Klis, M., & Mulder, C. H. (2008). Beyond the trailing spouse: The commuter partnership as an alternative to family migration. *Journal of Housing and the Built Environment, 23*(1), 1–19.

Vergés Bosch, N., & González Ramos, A. M. (2013). Beyond the work-life balance: Family and international mobility of the highly skilled. *Sociología y Tecnociencia, 3*(3), 55–76. http://diposit.ub.edu/dspace/handle/2445/111423

Vertovec, S. (2002). *Transnational networks and skilled labour migration.* Presented at the Ladenburger Diskurs "Migration" Gottlieb Daimler- und Karl Benz-Stiftung, Ladenburg. https://pure.mpg.de/rest/items/item_3012174/component/file_3012175/content.

Walsh, J. (2008). Navigating globalization: Immigration policy in Canada and Australia, 1945–2007 1. *Sociological Forum, 23*, 786–813. Wiley Online Library.

Weinar, A. (2018). Politics of emigration in Europe. In *The Routledge handbook of the politics of migration in Europe* (pp. 62–73). London: Routledge.

Weinar, A. (2019). *European citizenship and identity outside of the European Union.* London/New York: Routledge.

Weiner, M. (1995). *The global migration crisis: Challenge to states and to human rights.* New York: HarperCollins College Publishers.

Williams, A. M. (2007). International labour migration and tacit knowledge transactions: A multi-level perspective. *Global Networks, 7*(1), 29–50.

Williams, A., & Baláž, V. (2014). *International migration and knowledge.* London: Routledge.

Yao, L. (2012). *Highly skilled new Chinese migrants in the UK and the globalisation of China since 1990.* PhD thesis, The University of Manchester (United Kingdom).

Zahlan, A. B. (1982). *The Arab brain drain.* London: Ithaca Press.

Zhao, J., Drew, D., & Scott Murray, T. (2000). Brain drain and brain gain: The migration of knowledge workers from and to Canada. *Education Quarterly Review, 6*(3), 8.

Zolberg, A. (1999). Matters of state: Theorizing immigration policy. In *The handbook of international migration: The American experience* (pp. 71–93). New York: Russell Sage.

Chapter 3
The State and the Highly Skilled Immigrant

3.1 State Policies and Highly Skilled Migration

In the previous chapter we discussed the conceptualisations of the highly skilled and of skilled migration, and the related methodological traps. We also discussed the dominant role of the state in the definition of the highly skilled migrant. In this chapter we will discuss more closely the relationship between highly skilled migrants and the state, and the implications of that relationship for the migrants themselves. State policies not only open or close migration channels for the highly skilled, but they also shape the boundaries of the social field in which the individuals live their migration experience; cultural and social integration processes can be supported to a lesser or greater extent, opportunities for accompanying families can be developed, etc. Also, the opportunity structure for skills to wither or thrive is provided mainly by the country of destination, but the country of origin has its role to play in this part as well, e.g. by providing compatibility of its own education systems with the standards in countries of destination (Weinar 2017b).

In what follows we will discuss the role of both countries of destination and of origin in shaping the highly skilled migration space as potentially different from other migration spaces. We can say that migration space refers to a certain opportunity structure in which the highly skilled move across borders. Following the discussions in Chap. 2 on the underlying role of policies that shape the context of their mobility, highly skilled migrants can be seen as moving under specific circumstances and under specific rules. We will then move to the discussion of the migration experience of the highly skilled within this space. Throughout the chapter we will be paying particular attention to any differences in immigration policies for highly skilled migrants from one region of the world versus another. There are arguably different markets for highly skilled labor from the North and from the South, with those from the North often taking up different jobs from their counterparts from the South, mainly as regards industries and pay. Those from the North and

© The Author(s) 2020
A. Weinar, A. Klekowski von Koppenfels, *Highly-Skilled Migration: Between Settlement and Mobility*, IMISCOE Research Series, https://doi.org/10.1007/978-3-030-42204-2_3

from the South may also encounter different barriers on their path due to both exogenous and endogenous effects of "country labels". These distinctions have important integration implications, strongly suggesting that the integration processes of the highly skilled are neither homogenous nor necessarily significantly different from other migrant groups.

3.1.1   Why Countries Develop Highly Skilled Migration Policies

As noted in Chap. 2, interest in highly skilled migration and specially in the related public policies is split between two quite different streams: on the one hand, development scholars tend to focus on the impact of outward migration on less-developed countries of origin and what policies could mitigate this impact, with a shift in recent years toward migration and remittances as a positive force for development; on the other, economists and political scientists often look at the impact of highly skilled migration on the developed countries of destination, including impact on wages, and government policies put in place, for instance, to benefit the local economy.

This dual perspective complicates the task of researchers who try to make sense of the globally evolving trends on governance of the highly skilled migration. This complexity has been well analysed by Mathias Czaika, who edited the most comprehensive account on highly skilled migration policies and their drivers worldwide available to date (2018). In the introduction to the volume, Czaika presents the data on the rise of high-skilled migration policies globally between 2005 and 2015. He concludes that 68% of OECD high income countries developed such policies by 2015 (from 47% in 2005), 50% high income non-OECD countries (from 27% in 2005), 38% middle income countries (from 13% in 2005) and a booming 31% of low income countries (from just 8% in 2005). He notes that, "in 2015 half of the 172 UN member states declared an explicit interest in increasing the level of high-skilled migration either by attracting foreign or retaining native talent. This share has doubled since 2005, when 22% of all UN member states expressed this preference for additional high-skilled labour"(2018, p. 3). This assessment leads to a clearly bifurcated explanation of the drivers of this exponential growth.

In what follows we will consider highly skilled immigration policies developed by high income countries, and highly skilled emigration policies developed by lower income countries. Nonetheless, the presented bifurcation of policies does not mean that high-income countries do not engage in emigration policies, or that low income countries do not bid on the foreign talent. The divergence is rather a question of degree: return is not at the core of policies developed by high income countries, although they often have some innovative schemes (Rogers 1997; Sadowski-Smith and Li 2016; Weinar 2017a); while race for talent is not at the core of migration and development agenda of lower income countries, some attempt to lure foreign investment (and with it: foreign talent) exist (Gao et al. 2013; Fabry and Zeghni 2003; Kumar 2013).

3.1.1.1 Immigration Policies for Highly Skilled

On one hand, since at least the mid-1990s, Western industrialised countries have been leading the way towards knowledge-based economies, spearheading the global trend of immigration policies that should deliver the knowledge workers needed to support this economic transition (Czaika and Parsons 2017; Williams and Baláž 2014). In these economies, the rationale for specific policy choices included the ageing of their populations and related skill shortages in knowledge-intensive sectors (Basri and Box 2008; Kerr et al. 2016; Triandafyllidou and Isaakyan 2016).

Demographic and economic changes were not however limited only to these high income countries. Indeed, these changes have been felt also by the emerging economies (BRIC and developed Asian countries) albeit to a varied extent. These countries joined the race for talent in the last decade to assure the increases in productivity and further development (Kapur and McHale 2005a, b; Agrawal et al. 2011; Boeri et al. 2012). The advent of what Czaika calls the "global skills market" (2018) and Solimano calls the "global labour market" (2008) has changed the way governments select skilled migrants. The policy makers have adapted to these changes by taking into account the relative attractiveness of their country and highly-skilled migration offer (Czaika and Parsons 2017; Chiswick 2011; Basri and Box 2008; Wiesbrock and Hercog 2012). The most common policies include a special migration stream reserved for a target group of highly skilled migrants, defined on the basis of qualifications, i.e. educational attainment or professional profile, sometimes complemented by salary threshold requirement (see Chap. 2 for discussion). Such streams change and evolve constantly: the German residence permit for highly skilled system has been overhauled several times (Jurgens 2010; Werner 2002; Paul 2016), Canadian and Australian skilled worker point systems have been revamped on an almost yearly basis (Green and Green 1995; Knowles 2016; Wright 2015; Wright et al. 2016), while the Highly Skilled Migrant Programme in the UK has changed following the migration pressures after 2004 (Salt and Millar 2006), went through adjustments during the financial crisis, and will certainly change yet again after Brexit. Still, all immigration programs for the highly skilled usually consist of a series of elements, identified by McLaughlan and Salt (2002; see also Cerna and Czaika 2016). According to their findings, most of these programs offer simplified procedures for a work permit, especially if the migration flow is meant to address specific skill shortages (e.g. in IT or health sectors). Also, several schemes include a series of exemptions, e.g. from the labour market test (such as LMIA in Canada) or even the work permit tout court (e.g. for most intra-corporate transferees or posted workers). One of the more recent elements of these policies is the development of special paths to residency for foreign students, either foreseen as special fast-track procedures, or one to two years post-graduation grace periods for a job search. However, there is an important difference between the schemes offered by European Union countries and classic immigration countries[1]: the first offer strictly temporary stay (providing a pathway to permanency), while the latter offer both temporary and permanent skilled migration entry routes (McLaughlan and Salt 2002). To put it in more straightforward terms, the EU schemes focus more on the demand-side and are concerned with labour market outcomes of immigrant workers, to the detriment of their numbers, while the second type are mostly supply-driven, to accommodate the biggest possible numbers of highly-skilled people (often at the cost of their underemployment) (Czaika 2018; Koslowski 2014).

The changing landscape of highly skilled immigration policies from FDI-oriented to long-term development oriented means that an important shift has occurred with respect to one category of the highly-skilled migrant: in contrast to early writings (1990s–2000s), the category of "organisational expatriate" is more and more missing. While most states are still keen to support multinational companies in their internal professional mobility by designing special clauses for the intra-corporate transferees (Lavenex 2007; Lazarowicz 2013; Yost 1996), in the current economic and social context, in which policymakers seek to maximise their investment in immigration for the economic development, this stream has lost some of its allure. It is not big enough to impact the host economies, nor is it permanent enough to make a change in the workforce (Basri and Box 2008). By the virtue of Mode 4 of the General Agreement on Trade in Services (GATS),[2] these migrants do not enter the local labour market and they do not present an obvious value added for the policies designed to counteract demographic and economic transitions (but see OECD et al. 2004). As such, they are thus neither at the centre of the state policies, nor of key concern for business management policies, particularly considering the growing number of so-called "self-initiated expatriates" (Doherty 2013), as well as numerous others, who, as discussed in Chap. 2, often are not captured by official data on the highly skilled.

The policy competition exists, however, when the prize is the highly skilled international migrants, not bound by a multinational company, but constituting workforce to the local businesses. Classic immigration countries are at the forefront of policy innovation targeting this group. Koslowski (2014) attempted categorisation of these forerunners. He noted three models of highly skilled immigration policies: a "human capital" model based on state selection of permanent immigrants using a points system (in Canada); "neo-corporatist" model based on state selection using a point system with extensive business and labour participation (in Australia); and the market-oriented, demand-driven model based primarily on employer selection of migrants (in the US). Koslowski compared these systems as regards their

---

[1] Australia, Canada, New Zealand and the US.
[2] https://www.wto.org/english/tratop_e/serv_e/mouvement_persons_e/mouvement_persons_e.htm [acccessed 16 April 2019].

outcomes and concluded that the US system, based on H-1B temporary visas as the first channel of entry, attracted more highly skilled than the other two systems based on permanent immigration. Indeed, as the author noted, Canada and Australia had been expanding the temporary highly skilled migration schemes themselves. Aware of the ever-changing elements in this policy area, he noted that "the three ideal-typical selective migration policy models may soon become more historical arte-facts than actual descriptions of current government policy practice as the governments of each country move their policies toward other models" (p. 36).

Indeed, the analysis of highly skilled immigration policy trends is tricky, because in most countries the changes and tweaks of particular schemes occur so often that it is challenging to establish any long-term view or set models. What used to be a clear division even three decades ago, now seems to converge across the spectrum because of policy learning and subsequent policy convergence (Castles et al. 2014; Arcarazo and Geddes 2014; Facchini and Lodigiani 2014; Geddes 2018).

Despite these difficulties, some academic works do show how the countries fare in the field of highly skilled immigration schemes. In 2016, Lucie Cerna established an index of states' openness to high-skilled immigrants (so-called HSI Index) using OECD data and policy documents. She conducted an analysis that led to a policy ranking and their change between 2007 and 2012, taking into account admission mechanism and work permit rights composed of the following indicators: numerical caps, labour market test and labour protection, employer portability, spouse's work rights and permanent residency rights (Cerna 2016). Her main conclusion has been that the OECD countries tend to learn from each other and incrementally change their policies so they start to slowly converge. That work has been crucial to foster a better understanding of countries' position versus the highly skilled migration and it also confirms the convergence trends.

Considering this dynamic, several scholars sought to explain why countries still differ in their openness towards highly skilled migration. This topic has grown in saliency amidst the discussion about migration policies in developed countries in general. How the details of these policies are developed is a question that can be answered looking through a domestic or an international lens. Domestically, in the demand-driven systems, the employers and their interest that mostly define the tar-get group for highly skilled policies (Hercog and Sandoz 2018; Kerr et al. 2016; Kolbe and Kayran 2019). Even in supply-driven systems, the voiced needs of employers are taken into account (Knowles 2016). In consequence, the tools used to select highly skilled migrants are not uniform across countries and depend both on the local labour market and the national definition of "talent" and "skill" (see Chap. 2 for a more in-depth discussion). Lucie Cerna offered more insights on how these processes actually occur and why the outcomes differ so much. In looking at the case of the highly skilled, she applied the general migration policy models that explain migration policy making (Cerna 2009, 2016). She proposed a comparative political economy framework to consider the development (or not) of the high-skilled immigration policies in advanced industrial economies. She found differ-ences between national policies despite the seemingly converging policy objectives to admit more highly skilled migrants to fill labour shortages in key sectors. Her work has brought to light the role that different coalitions – between high-skilled labour, low-skilled labour and capital – play in shaping the policy outcomes and that these outcomes have little to do with the overarching economic interest or goal, but rather with the strength of these coalitions (Lodge 2006; Gawrich et al. 2010).

Another view on how the policies are developed comes from the policy learning perspective on the international level. First insights to this approach came from the field of European integration studies. The idea of policy emulation is inherent to the idea of Europeanisation (Börzel and Risse 2012). Policies concerning highly skilled migration are no different. In the context of the European Union, the perceived risk of losing the talent to the classic countries of immigration opened the door to a significant increase in policy learning and policy development on both national and European levels. More specifically, by 2008, more than half of 27 member states had some sort of clearly developed policy toward highly skilled migrants (EMN 2013; Cerna 2009). The post-communist Eastern European states were over-represented among those states which had not yet developed such policies (Kloc-Nowak 2013; Kaczmarczyk et al. 2012), mainly because the industries that would need highly skilled workers remained underdeveloped in this region. At the same time, the discussion among member states at the EU level on the Directive on migration of highly skilled workers (which became the so-called Blue Card) gave them the opportunity to look critically at their own solutions and think about other possibilities. The so-called Blue Card Directive was approved in May 2009, after long negotiations that juxtaposed national interests and policy-making traditions with domestic definitions of the highly skilled (Cerna 2013a). The impact of this supranational initiative was felt most strongly in the countries that did not have a clear highly skilled migration mechanism prior to 2009, meaning that the Blue Card filled an important policy gap (Cerna 2013b). Similar dynamics can be seen in other regions of the world. As early as 2000, Iredale considered similarities in migration policy patterns in the Asia-Pacific region (Iredale 2000). More recently, the work of several scholars has brought to light policy convergence in both Latin America (Acosta 2018; Arcarazo and Geddes 2014; Acosta and Freier 2018) and South-East Asia (Kaur 2018).

3.1.1.2 Policies Targeting Brain Drain and Brain Gain

While receiving countries focus on attracting highly skilled migrants, the oft-stated goal of the policies of the countries of origin is counteracting "brain drain" and investing in "brain gain". "Brain drain" and "brain gain" are two concepts that are crucial to the literature on highly skilled migrants, particularly within the field of economics and development studies.

The brain drain debates dominated the scholarly exchanges during the 1960s and 1970s (Zahlan 1981; Bhagwati and Rodriguez 1975; Glaser and Christopher Habers 1978; Docquier and Marfouk 2006), focusing on the detrimental effects of emigration on development of the countries then referred to as "Third World" countries. Scholars, mainly in economics, brought up evidence of disproportionate loss of public funds were spent on education of specialists who later on chose to emigrate and did not bring expected return on investment to the country. Also, they were looking at the emigration of those educated abroad, as lost potential. These debates were subsequently complemented by "brain gain" debates (Cohen and Kranz 2015; Docquier and Rapoport 2012; Stark and Simon Fan 2007; Commander et al. 2004). Scholars of "brain gain" noted that effects of emigration on the country of origin are multifaceted and complex, and cannot be measured in win-lose binary opposition. This hypothesis suggests that emigration can still have a positive effect on development in the country of origin, considering that human capital of emigrants might be better used abroad (with access to better technologies and superior research environments) and not lost at home (e.g.in the case of unstable political and economic environment), also known as "brain waste". This approach has been defined as "modernisation of emigration" (Portes and Celaya 2013) (Box 3.1).

Box 3.1: Does Migration Pay Off?
It is a question asked also by economists, whose approach is less individualised than that of sociologists, and rely on large datasets. Assirelli et al. (2019) looked at the labour market outcomes for highly skilled migrants from Italy during the Eurozone crisis. They applied multivariate analyses to a 2011 cohort and showed that young people from upper-class families, foreign citizens, graduates in scientific and internationally oriented fields, and best-performing students are more likely to migrate. Moreover, compared to the "stayers," graduate migrants enjoy more favorable outcomes in terms of wages, unemployment risks, access to skilled employment, and career satisfaction. These results support the thesis of "modernisation of migration."

Scholars have also suggested that new knowledge and skills developed abroad can be brought to the country of origin through professional networks, return or remittances. More concretely, this school of the "new economics of brain drain" (Brzozowski 2008) indicates that countries of origin may gain from the emigration of skilled workers in six ways:

- Positive effect of induced education (Lucas 2005; Stark et al. 1997; Mountford 1997; Beine et al. 2001; Schiff 2005).
- This "brain gain" dynamics is explained as an impact of the perspective of emigration on the propensity to pursue education at home. If it is easier to emigrate with a certain type of a diploma in hand or with a certain level of education, more young people would flock to get these credentials. However, the argument goes, as not all of them can emigrate, the country is left with a larger skill pool that impacts positively its development.
- Return migration (Stark and Simon Fan 2007) is a positive force for development, as it brings various forms of new capital (human, financial or social) back to the country of origin and stimulates economic and social progress.
- Remittances (Ratha 2005; Ghosh 2006), i.e. financial transfers from emigrants to the country of origin towards their families or towards their own investments, constitute in many cases a large part of the GDP and thus can boost the economic growth.

- Diaspora effects (Kugler and Rapoport 2005; Breschi et al. 2017) are the influences the emigrants have through their professional and social networks on their societies in the countries of origin. This phenomenon is known also as knowledge transfer, which "in organizations is the process through which one unit (e.g., group, department, or division) is affected by the experience of another" (Argote and Ingram 2000: 15).
- Trade effects (Felbermayr and Toubal 2012; Flisi and Murat 2011), which can include both increased bilateral trade and increased FDI and include also increased bilateral trade and FDIs. Indeed, the highly skilled migrants have been found to reduce information-related risks for investment.

The "brain gain" theories have been both embraced by policymakers worldwide under the migration for development agenda (De Haas 2010) and criticised by economists on the empirical grounds (Faini 2007; Brzozowski 2008). The "brain gain" theory seems to apply in specific circumstances to specific groups. In fact, some scholars observed that especially highly skilled migrants do not remit as much as low skilled migrants, because they tend to invest in their new country of residence rather than back in the country of origin (Faini 2007). Moreover, it is difficult to measure the educational dividend because many migrants leave the country without a diploma pursuing education abroad instead. Finally, as it is the case with most research in economics, most scholars focus on long-term and permanent skilled migrants, and generally do not include temporary movements in their analysis, while important share of skilled migration is temporary or circular. As regards diaspora effects, some scholars uncovered its complex nature, and found evidence of a varied effects among various ethnic groups. Finally, the idea that highly skilled migration has a greater impact on the country of origin through the flow of FDIs and growing trade has been also challenged (cfr. Brzozowski 2008).

Regardless of the inconclusive results on "brain gain," governments have invested in emigration policies (Weinar 2017a, b, 2019). These policies consist of schemes promoting circular mobility and return of highly skilled migrants, to contain "brain drain" and/or to boost "brain gain". Middle income and low income countries have been most active in developing this type of skilled migration programs. The reasoning is the same as in the highly developed countries: the need to support economic development in the future world of knowledge economy, and in many cases also demographic pressures that can hinder that development. This is especially true for Eastern European countries that experience adverse effects of ageing while faced with fast-paced development pressures (Davoudi et al. 2010; Hoff 2011). This is often paired with impossibility of attracting highly skilled immigrants from other countries due to fierce global competition. A large number of developing countries have adopted "migration for development" policy agenda in the last two decades and have since engaged in policies that would focus on return and retention of their own highly skilled citizens (Rogers 1997; De Haas 2010; Shima 2010; Agunias 2008; Wickramasekara 2003). This idea goes beyond the use of remittances for development, especially since we know that highly skilled migrants tend to remit less than low-skilled ones, and instead focus on various forms of "brain gain" or "brain circulation" (Schiff 2005; Harvey 2012; Jöns 2009; Saxenian 2005; Tung 2008). The policies on circulation and return of the highly skilled emigrants are usually divided in those encouraging temporary return (or even virtual return, often for training purposes) and those encouraging permanent return.

Temporary return is usually a return for less than 12 months. The most common length of such return varies between a few days to up to 6 months. One particular subset of temporary return would be circular return, with the returnee spending a set number of days in the home country over a number of years (usually the length of the program, 2–4 years). Policies of temporary return encompass two sets of initiatives that accompany the migrant: initiatives that trigger the decision to return and initiatives that support the migrant in the temporary reintegration throughout the period of temporary return.

Another set of policies are those of permanent return, which encompass three sets of initiatives that support the migrants at each of the three stages of return: initiatives that trigger the decision to return; initiatives that support reintegration in the first 6–12 months; initiatives that support retention after the initial period of reintegration. In this context, state-assisted return programmes (SARPs) (Cohen and Kranz 2015) for the highly-skilled focus on repatriation of the desirable human capital by providing assistance to returnees and their families. At first glance, they do not differ from SARPs which are conceived for other categories of migrants, however, the difference lies in the way they are implemented. They usually are limited in scope, implemented in targeted partnerships with a limited number of stakeholders deemed the best placed to appeal to the highly skilled returnees; they tend to have higher funding, often sustained for longer periods of time; and they include hard and soft measures that are limited to the target group in demand. They focus more on the recognition and appraisal of skills, qualifications and experience to facilitate the brain-gain dynamics in the home economy (see discussions in Sinatti 2015; Sadowski-Smith and Li 2016; Koh 2015).

In contrast to the highly skilled immigration policies, emigration policies have not been a focus of any ranking or serious academic analysis that would attempt categorisations or models. This might be because these policies are relatively new and very similar, supported by international organisations (such as World Bank, UNDP or International Organisation for Migration). In this sense the international dimension of policy creation is more important than the domestic coalitions. In many SARPs the government designs an initiative on its own and seeks support from external partners, such as immigrant organisations and businesses experiencing labour shortages (Shima 2010; Klagge and Klein-Hitpass 2010; Siddiqui and Tejada 2014). However, the core of policy learning comes from the international level with many global initiatives supporting exchange best practice and experience.[3] Policy convergence stems from this exposure to international field (Weinar 2010), while the role of domestic coalitions has not been studied so far.

---

[3] See e.g. the Migration4Development initiative http://www.migration4development.org/ [accessed 12 April 2019].

3.2   Measuring Policy Effects: Many Faces of Success and Failure

How do the policies targeting the highly skilled fare in achieving their goals? The question does not have just one answer, again going back to definitions – here, it is the definition of success of each of these policies, which is highly context-related. While some policies will aim at getting the largest number of highly skilled people to fill in temporary jobs in a particular industry, others will want them to settle and contribute to the society in a more holistic way. While some will target specific professions and skill-sets, other will keep these options open, looking on the wholeness of human capital that is coming in. In some cases the endgame might not be necessarily the attraction of the highly skilled migrant *per se*, as in the case of the Blue Card, which aim is to create a level-playing field within the EU internal market. Moreover, judging from constant changes to the schemes in virtually all the countries, it may seem that at least highly skilled immigration policies are under political scrutiny and thus constantly adapted to achieve better, or different, policy outcomes.

The academic big-scale assessments elaborated to date have not attempted getting into the nuances of setting context-based policy targets. To achieve comparative pool of policy solutions, the indicators must be harmonised, what usually leads to less detail, but allows for a bigger picture to emerge. Consequently, scholars who attempt a measurement of success or failure usually use the number of highly skilled migrants attracted by a specific scheme as an indicator of success. Koslowski (2014) compared the numbers of highly skilled attracted as permanent and temporary residents to draw his conclusion on the efficacy of Canadian, Australian and US models (see above). Czaika and Parsons (2017) also define success as the volume of highly skilled human capital attracted by a policy, yet they go much more into detail on how various elements of the policy can work towards this goal. They combine annual bilateral data on labor flows of highly skilled immigrants for 10 OECD destinations between 2000 and 2012 and juxtapose them towards new databases of unilateral and bilateral policy instruments. They conclude, quite differently from Koslowski, that points-based systems are much more effective in attracting and selecting high-skilled migrants than employer-driven European and US schemes, but they agree than permanent immigration offers are less attractive to highly skilled than temporary immigration schemes, while they do attract less skilled migrants. They also underline the importance of the bilateral recognition of diploma and social security agreements to improve the selectivity of immigrant flows.

As regards emigration policies towards highly skilled, their effectiveness measured by the numbers of returnees is largely contested in literature (Sinatti 2015; Cohen and Kranz 2015). Unfortunately, there is not enough independent research to draw conclusions on these policies. From what we know, the return and reintegration of the highly skilled depends on the same elements as the policies that attract them: additional bilateral agreements, recognition of qualifications, and skill-relevant employment.

Indeed, we should look beyond the numbers to laud a success of a public policy. If the ultimate objective to invite the highly skilled migrant is to contribute to the economic growth, new knowledge-based economy and social development, it is indeed important to consider social, economic and cultural dimension of migrant's arrival. In other words, the real measure of success in our opinion is not the attracted volume of human capital, but its full utilisation both on the labour market and in all other spheres of social life. The issues of over-skilling and under-employment, as well as failed social and cultural integration are thus of primordial importance to the policy impact. In this section we will discuss the effects of policies from this perspective: what are the supports and barriers to the contribution of the highly skilled migrants to the countries of residence, both at immigration and return? Are there any specific groups that are especially vulnerable or especially privileged in their journey? We subscribe here to the observation by Hercog and Sandoz (2018) who state that:

Migration governance needs to be approached holistically, encompassing not only admission and integration policies, but also skill recognition policies, labour market policies and higher education programmes. Altogether, the interplay between policies, discourses and practices influences the composition of immigration flows and guides potential skilled migrants to particular privileges in society. As the historical approach shows us, privileges may also be taken away. Hence, the category of highly skilled migrants is constantly negotiated and contested and can only be used as a category of practice. (Hercog and Sandoz 2018, p. 7).

This approach puts the migrant experience at the centre of examination. In what follows, we will thus turn to the analysis of integration challenges experienced by highly skilled migrants. We will consider how migrants make use of and contest the opportunity structure shaped by macro-level (government policies) and meso-level (organisations and networks) to arrive at their life goals.

3.2.1 Labour Market and Professional Life: Two-Level Approach

Migration of a highly skilled migrant is sometimes depicted through the metaphors of "rucksack" and "treasure chest" (Erel 2010, p. 649). The first metaphor reflects the economic theories of human capital, where the migrant is seen as a rather passive actor in the migration journey and their cultural capital is seen as a constant and not very flexible tool that can fit or not fit the labour market at the destination. The content of the "rucksack" cannot be changed, however, the owner of the rucksack can go to other places, where it can be more appreciated. If it is not, then the choice is rather simple: the emigrant needs to throw away the content and look for a new one (Box 3.2).

Box 3.2: Human and Social Capital

Pierre Bourdieu argued that, if we are to understand our social interactions more completely, then we must broaden our understanding of "capital" beyond being only the economic. Looking at human, cultural and social capital enable us to arrive at a better understanding of the value individuals put into circulation in society, and the value attributed to them.

Cultural capital is broadly understood as the knowledge and cultural competence which a person holds.

Human capital, a broader concept, is usually understood as the formal education and training which a person has, over his or her life, accumulated.

Social capital, finally, derives from the networks in which a person is embedded. These might be as diverse as university alumni/ae associations, villages, families or employees of a large multi-national company.

Bourdieu argued that each of these forms of capital, applied in a market setting, would translate into economic capital. In short, these forms of capital also have innate value. It is this value which is recognized in highly-skilled worker programs.

We can see how, in an international setting, all three of these forms of capital have value, yet the possibilities for misinterpretation and undervaluing are numerous. Assumptions concerning country of origin – Global South – might, for instance, reduce the value of human capital.

In contrast, the Bourdieusian concept of capital is closer to the metaphor of a" treasure chest", where the treasures consist of three types of cultural capital: incorporated (mental schemes, language, values, results of socialisation), institutional (formal qualifications and skills), and symbolic (cultural objects valued in a given culture) (Bourdieu 1986). In the case of immigrants, it is usually the first two types of cultural capital that are taken into consideration. They are assessed, whether implicitly or explicitly, by a potential migrant, who designs a migration strategy around them. In many cases the individual indeed looks for the closest fit possible (e.g. emigration to a country they speak the language of, or they have credentials from), but it is not always the case. After arrival, these "treasures" are put out in the open and allowed to be valued by the host labour market. In the process, the migrant engages in the negotiation of the value of the cultural capital they bring.

From the migrant's perspective, the labour market outcomes in migration are to a large extent determined by, what we might call "hard" and "soft barriers" to labour market integration. The "hard barriers" are all policies that control the entry process: visa policy, work permit schemes, labour migration quotas etc. In the case of the highly skilled who qualify for the dedicated entry channels, these hard barriers are lowered or withdrawn altogether, and their entry is thus facilitated. Nevertheless, the mere act of entry to a territory with no hard barriers does not guarantee positive labour entry outcomes. The key element to the success defined in this way is the dynamics of "soft barriers" to labour market integration.

These barriers exist for all migrant workers, on all skill levels, but in the case of the highly skilled they are crucial to maintain the good quality of the human capital that is brought to the labour market in question. Umut Erel calls them "nationally-based protectionism" and in fact, they serve as an additional layer protecting the domestic workforce (Erel 2010). Scholars have identified a number of factors that impede highly skilled workers to achieve their full potential in the host country: a lack of language skills, the non-recognition of foreign credentials, and a lack of country-specific knowledge and job experiences. In most cases, these barriers are not fully removed or are removed only for some groups. In fact, a lack of a soft barrier can be an opportunity structure, giving some migrants a privileged access to the labour market. This is the case in the contexts where countries of origin and destination have privileged bilateral relations as regards language, qualifications recognition and generalised knowledge of each other's work cultures. This is for example the case of the UK and Commonwealth countries, Quebec and France, and to a lesser extent the European Union countries. If too difficult to remove, these barriers are responsible for the phenomena of brain waste, over-skilling and underemployment. Soft barriers effectively limit the rights of the migrant worker, meaning the full access to the labour market, access to social rights and decent work. Facilitated access to the labour market, even on the pair with natives (i.e. without the labour market test) is not a guarantee of an access to the decent work or to the social rights, or mobility rights within the labour market (as it is the case in European Union). Ideally, migrant workers let into the labour market should be able to change jobs and move up the ladder if their skills and experience allow them to. Yet, in many jurisdictions that apply the demand-driven policies, the barriers to access to social rights can incentivize a migrant to stay put with one employer, while barriers to recognition of qualifications can block any advancement to a better-paying job.

Both hard and soft barriers are present on the migrant's path to integration. Even if highly skilled migrants usually have less of an issue with hard barriers, soft barriers determine the success of their migration project. In what follows we discuss the soft barriers which migrants face on two levels: macro-level and meso-level. We follow here the conceptualisation of Schittenhelm and Schmidtke (2011). Macro-level is where the more formal requirements rest and where the exogenous country labels play out. The characteristics that are endogenous to the country are not mere perceptions, they are rather components of a migrant's "treasure chest". They can underpin a "country label" but are measurable, such as level and quality of education, social and cultural development, migrants' health levels. Therefore, on the macro-level a migrant needs to address challenges to their cultural capital posed by formal/administrative/regulatory frameworks, outside of immigration policies. On the meso-level, a migrant has to face challenges related to perceptions about their cultural capital. The characteristics exogenous to the country, or what might be called the "country label", is a set of beliefs existing in any given host country vis-à-vis a country of origin and its citizens. These beliefs can result in subconscious bias in the host country towards one group, but also in ungrounded overtly positive attitudes towards another group, regardless of the migrant's skill level. They can influence migrants ability to progress on the labour market and lead a successful professional career.

3.2.1.1 Macro-level Challenges

On the macro-level, migrants navigate the institutional framework to keep value of their formal qualifications and skills. In their long-term comparison of Canadian and the US system for admitting economic immigrants, Somerville and Walsworth observed that permanent immigrants to Canada have been increasingly over-skilled and underemployed, while the situation was much better for the immigrants in the US. Their main explanation of this discrepancy was that the Canadian point system makes skilled immigrants vulnerable to several risk factors after arrival. First and foremost, foreign credentials and work experience are systematically discounted by Canadian employers (Somerville and Walsworth 2009). Their findings are consistent with a long-standing explanation of why immigrants face these difficulties: already two decades ago the researchers noted that there is no return for foreign experience and foreign education has a lower return than Canadian education (Schaafsma and Sweetman 2001; Buzdugan and Halli 2009). The now notorious concept of "Canadian experience," i.e. the work experience in the Canadian labour market with a Canadian employer, haunts more recent cohorts of economic skilled immigrants (Slade et al. 2005). This has reached the point that many government and non-government organisations took notice and now provide internship programs that would help these workers improve their CVs. However, the system does not shield newcomers from decreasing their income level, regardless of the fact that they usually hold degrees and experience in the most well-paid fields, e.g. engineering, physical sciences, and commerce. However they all were the most underpaid relative to native-born Canadians (Anisef et al. 2003). According to the results demonstrated by Somerville and Walsworth, the issues of recognition and related over-skilling and underemployment did not materialise so dramatically in the US system, which is demand-driven. The authors suggested that there is not a great difference in acceptance of foreign credentials and experience in the US compared to Canada. However, the very nature of the point system implies embedded discrepancies and information, because the federal government is not allowed to give different weight to credentials coming from different national jurisdictions. The authors cite an example of a chartered accounting designation earned in India, which in 2008, under the federally-run point system awarded up to 25 points required for admission (almost 40 % of all points), thus increasing the chance of applicant and signaling that this professional designation is valued at the labour market in Canada. Upon arrival, however, the professional designation is not recognised automatically and has zero value unless it is recognised by the provincial professional body in charge of recognition of such qualifications. A chartered accounting designation earned in India is often not recognised and the immigrant has to go through years of additional costly training to prove his or her abilities and knowledge. On the contrary, such a credential earned in the UK would be more easily accepted, and in the specific case of French credentials in Quebec, the procedure would be swift and less costly (Beck and Weinar 2017).

According to Somerville and Walsworth, in the US case, immigrants had to go through the recruitment process from abroad, and thus they would come with a job offer in hand. Those, whose credentials or experience were not recognised or diminished, would not receive the job offer. Moreover, if the job offer was not meeting their expectations, these immigrants would not accept it. The process of pre-selection was thus more efficient in the US system. Still, the US economic immigration program is substantially smaller than the Canadian program, and the immigrants coming through all other routes as well as through the H-1B visa program face the same obstacles to labour market mobility and success as permanent immigrants in Canada.

The results presented by these authors give us a hint to what barriers on the macro-level migrants face when trying to access the labour market. We can thus extrapolate the following issues related to the value of the cultural capital brought by a skilled migrant:

- Difficult access to recognition of professional qualifications: highly skilled migrants everywhere have difficulties getting their professional qualifications in regulated professions recognised. They are thus, essentially, barred from exercising their profession. Obtaining recognition of foreign-acquired professional qualifications is a complex undertaking for immigrants, particularly for recent arrivals. Even when the labour market seems to be open for highly skilled workers, its internal structure of certifications and professional recognitions forms a dense net of barriers not only to employment but a decent life. Even when the correct authority is found, recognition is hardly guaranteed. Depending on the country in which the qualification was earned, the language spoken by the applicant, and a plethora of other factors, many migrants with foreign-earned qualifications find themselves holding rather worthless pieces of paper once they reach their destination (Desiderio and Weinar 2014; Schuster et al. 2013). In a way, the internal, "invisible" obstacles serve to prioritise employment of "natives" and improve their chance on the labour market.
- "Country labelling" embedded in the institutional system: professional bodies responsible for recognition procedure have limited exposure to foreign credentials and thus have little understanding of their value. Usually, the credentials from countries in the same region or in the same political and economic space (like OECD) get more understanding and positive feedback. There are however credentials earned in countries which bring about negative associations and suspicions regarding quality and translatability of education, and thus recognition requires more time and effort. In the same vein, they push migrants to stick to the sectors and occupations where the demand for cheaper labour is the highest causing underemployment and brain waste (Mattoo et al. 2005; Sumption 2013; Pires 2015). There is in effect a glass ceiling, which has perpetuated the duality of the labour market well into the twenty-first century for migrants with mid- to high-skills (Piore 1970).
- Institutional setting limiting the information flow: national authorities which remove hard barriers to immigration of the highly skilled migrants usually do not have the prerogative to remove the soft barriers. They also do not usually give precise information on each individual situation, what reduces opportunities for making informed decision by migrants themselves.

Macro-level policy solutions to the macro-level issues can be found through bilateral cooperation on the state level. The Mutual Recognition Agreements (MRAs) are the prime example on how the states of origin and destination can make access to the labour market less painful and prevent brain waste in the longer run. They are agreements that set standard rules for the recognition of credentials and access to the professional practice that apply to all individuals who obtained their qualifications in a signatory country. The agreements bind the regulatory bodies which enter into an MRA to value the same qualification issued by the same authority in the partner country at any time. MRAs are negotiated through a lengthy and meticulous process of curriculum comparison and translation of learning outcomes. In doing so, MRAs improve transparency and consistency of recognition procedures for participating countries. The success of this process depends on the coordinating ability of the respective governments. The negotiations of the sectoral MRAs between France and Quebec provides a prime example of when governments played this role successfully (Beck and Weinar 2017). In addition, MRAs often include simplified procedures for the recognition of qualifications obtained in participating countries, as compared to the general rules applying for all other foreign qualifications. More fundamentally, in economically integrated regional areas the conclusion and implementation of MRAs serve broader economic and political objectives than that of facilitating the international portability of foreign qualifications per se. That is, they support the provision of intra-regional liberalisation and, in some cases, also of workers' mobility, as it is the case in the European Union (Blitz 1999; Currie 2016).

3.2.1.2 Meso-level Challenges

While macro-level can pose obstacles and offer solutions in terms of broader institutional framework, the meso-level influences employability of a highly-skilled migrant in a different way, mostly through access to employment networks. The employers are crucial for the individual success, and they can support the success of the macro-level policies, as in the case of the US economic immigrant program. However, in many cases there are more obstacles that they actually put in the way of the immigrant when it comes to finding employment on their skill level. The problems derive from the widespread negative perceptions regarding the credentials and professional experience completed abroad, or subconscious bias towards certain ethnic or national groups (Bauder 2005).

To be fair, there is evidence to suggest that there is a gap and variance regarding quality of foreign credentials and professional experience. Research shows that in some cases the title of the credential might be the same, but the content of the study and related skills are not (Sweetman 2004; Li and Sweetman 2014; Aumüller 2016). Yet, the prejudice is more accentuated in the case of immigrants coming from either non-English speaking or non-Western countries. Somerville and Walsworth noted that Canadian employers tend to impose a discriminatory income penalty on minorities (see also Basran and Zong 1998). Authors refer to the research that used longitudinal Canadian Census data comparing skilled immigrants' earnings to earnings of native-born workers with similar credentials. They conclude that in the last three decades the salary hiatus has been growing (Grant and Sweetman 2004; Li 2003; Picot and Sweetman 2004). This has occurred in the period of the growing diversity of immigration to Canada, where American and European immigrants have ceased their place to immigrants from Asia and Africa. The question of "translatability" of qualifications is thus crucial, well beyond the Canadian case. Indeed, Sardana et al. observed that Chinese and Indian highly skilled immigrants in South Australia faced clear discrimination on the labour market related to their foreign qualifications (Sardana et al. 2016). Benson-Rea and Rawlinson also confirm that Australian employers were often unwilling to recognize foreign qualifications obtained in a developing country as being on a par with local qualifications obtained in a developed nation (Benson-Rea and Rawlinson 2003). The immigrants coming from developing and non-Anglo-Saxon countries were perceived by employers as being less productive, more expensive (cost of training on organisational culture, country-specific social skills etc.) and overall more difficult to integrate into the workforce (lack of soft skills and different relationship values) (Syed 2008).

Meso-level is not only about employers, it is also about available network support. As they maneuver the legal and policy implications of moving their skills abroad, immigrants use the resources available to them through the support networks, which are crucial for information and valorisation of the "treasure chest" (Bauder 2005). In the case of highly skilled migrants, the networks can be of two kinds: traditional ethnic/national networks, and more often: professional networks (Tilly 2007). Social networks can be career-enhancing or binding. The first type provides support and value to the cultural capital of an immigrant. They support the migrant in job search, counteract deskilling and in general are connected to a wider social context of the receiving society or international professional networks. Binding social networks, on the other hand, can be translated into the type of ethnic enclaves built mostly around low-skilled occupations. They offer support and lower general risks of migration, but in the case of the highly skilled are often the reason behind underemployment, because they cannot connect the skilled migrant to the outer labour market, where such skills are sought for, nor can they help them remove the soft barriers to employment or adapt skills to the new labour market (Schüller 2016; Ojo and Shizha 2018). They also do not counteract what Thondhlana et al. (2016) called "warehouse mentality," i.e. the focus on any employment, instead of the right employment. In the case of the Zimbabwean highly skilled immigrants in the UK described by Thondhlana et al., a recurring theme was thus the immobilizing aspect of non-highly skilled non-professional community as it did not offer resources that promote immediate entry into professional jobs. In the same vein, one of the reasons for failure of highly skilled Canada-bound economic immigrants on the labour market, according to Somerville (2015), was their limited access to networks. Indeed, her research shows that they did not have access to information about the risks and roadblocks towards successful labour market integration on the same level as the US-bound immigrants had prior to arrival. Kin networks to which the Canada-bound immigrants referred had little reliable information about the potential perils of immigration, while professional networks open to international professionals from various ethnic and national groups are not that well developed (Somerville 2015).

Nurturing networks can support migrant's search for employment providing information about posts that could lead to the further development in professional area, regardless of the soft barriers to be removed. The scope of binding networks is too general to readily offer this type of specialised advice. It is the choice of the migrant to what kind of network they will anchor. The right choice of the network and support structure on the meso-level is crucial for success on the macro-level (removal of soft-barriers).

Schittenhelm and Schmidtke (2011) have shown that meso-level challenges have long-term impacts on migrants and their descendants. In the study, the researchers examined the careers of highly skilled immigrants in Canada and Germany, with degrees in three professional fields: medicine, engineering, and management. The immigrants were categorised according to macro-level variables, i.e. their educational titles (received abroad or in the host country) and residence permits. They were also grouped according to their social embeddedness, to reflect the meso-level. The research showed that the professional trajectories of migrants in the labour market are not simply determined in one given stage; rather, they undergo different stages and are subject to long- and short-term effects. Short-term effects were felt by the immigrant, while the long-term effects were felt even by the second generation. The study uncovered the process by which cumulative disadvantages experienced by the skilled migrants at the beginning of his journey resulted in an increase in inequality over time. Both in Germany and in Canada the challenges to successful application of the cultural capital were similar for the immigrant during the immediate transition phase. Issues of recognition of qualifications, underemployment or over-skilling were rampant, mostly due to the inefficiencies in the meso-level. Moreover, in the European context, the researchers discovered distinct patterns of social and symbolic exclusion over time, with underachievement reproduced well into the second generation, again due to the meso-level. This was especially the case of non-Western immigrants (Schittenhelm and Schmidtke 2011).

The results of studies analysing the meso-level challenges allow us to extrapolate several issues that highly skilled migrants must confront when accessing the labour market:

– Subconscious or conscious bias of employers fed by exogenous country labels. This bias leads employers to distrust qualification, skills or work ethics, even if formally they have been acknowledged as equal to natives. This bias can also work in favour of some groups: we will discuss this in more detail in Chap. 4.
– Limited access to native professional networks outside of the ethnic/national group. This is the case with many highly skilled migrants from the Global South, who have limited access to opportunity structures favouring mobility. Migrants from Global North in general have more exposure to non-ethnic professional networks and their situation can differ: this is tackled in more depth in Chap. 4.

There are a few meso-level solutions to meso-level barriers. In fact, these issues can be tackled through public education campaigns and through people-to-people contacts. The difficulty to apply policy solutions top-down, leads migrants to find different ways of coping with them.

Some scholars have brought to light the importance of the way the "treasure chest" is viewed by the migrants themselves. In this sense, we cannot conceptually separate immigrant from his country of origin, as the cultural capital is built in the certain habitus, denoted by social and cultural norms, beliefs and values (Bourdieu 2017). The way skills are defined, acquired and valorised in the country of origin influences the future activities and gestures the immigrants will perform on the host labour market. The habitus of origin defines how the immigrants perceive their skills and their position on the new labour market (Bauder 2005). These views may change after exposure to the host country social norms, values, and beliefs about skills. In a way, this is the recognition and acknowledgment of the exogenous and endogenous country labelling at play by the migrants themselves, which leads to a variety of adaptation strategies.

This aspect has been studied by Nowicka, who examined the narratives and practices regarding labour market performance of skilled and highly skilled Polish immigrants in the UK. On the surface, these migrants faced no soft barriers to employment on macro-level, as EU framework assures recognition of educational attainment. However, the gap between home education and the host education blocked them from working on their nominal skill level. They also were bound by the meso-level ethnic networks. Nowicka identified two complementary strategies that the migrants used to deal with this situation (Nowicka 2014). First, the narrative on "useless higher education," which served as an explanation of underemployment or over-skilling of all her interviewees. All the respondents felt that the Polish educational system values general education and knowledge, but does not provide practical labour market skills needed to succeed in the British labour market at their skill level. They still valued Polish education, as giving more illuminated view of the world, its history, culture and politics, but conceded it to the private sphere. Second, in the work sphere, Polish skilled migrants only used this set of non-practical skills to impress the employers as intelligent and possibly able to perform more complex tasks than other low-skilled workers, building thus employer's trust and soliciting the opportunity to learn new practical skills and thus enter the outer labour market with credible skilled experience. Nowicka conceptualises this adaptive strategy as "migration skills". These are skills related to general education that are used only in the context of migration to improve one's standing on the labour market. This strategy can be called negotiation between macro- and meso-levels.

However, the interaction between the macro and meso-levels can, in some cases, create a specific opportunity structure, in which also non-Western immigrants find professional success. Thondhlana et al. (2016) describe the cases of Zimbabwean highly skilled immigrants who chose to come to the United Kingdom. The macro-level was crucial to their professional development, as they were able to come through schemes such as the UK Highly Skilled Migrant Programme. Their strength was British-styled education and many years of UK-relevant work experience. Zimbabwe, being a Commonwealth country, has several joint professional programs with UK-based organisations that regulate professions, such as the UK

Institute of Engineers. This means that Zimbabwean engineers graduating from these programs become automatically members of the organisation and they don't need to go through the procedure of recognition of qualifications. With this qualification and work experience, the subjects of the study could secure a position in the UK and immigrate as a relocated staff (Thondhlana et al. 2016).

These two cases show that employing strategically the macro-level opportunity can remove barriers to labour market integration for migrants at risk of extreme "country labelling" on meso-level. In fact, the Polish skilled migrants from Nowicka's study, white Europeans with all opportunities offered by intra-EU mobility, did not achieve the same level of professional development as some of the African migrants.

3.2.1.3   Facing Soft Barriers in Return Migration

We must say that there is limited academic literature on the topic of labour market integration of returnees. The dominant literature has been produced on the occasion of various international cooperation projects (Hercog and Siegel 2011; Van Houte and Davids 2008; Van Houte et al. 2015; Koser and Kuschminder 2015; Kuschminder 2014). Still, from what we have seen, the issues regarding the use and negotiation of cultural capital acquired abroad do not disappear in the case of returning highly skilled emigrants. The macro-level obstacles to recognition of qualifications hurt immigrants and emigrants the same (Wickramasekara 2003), when the country of origin does not recognise automatically foreign credentials: e.g. returning Canadian students with foreign medical degree are treated in the same way as immigrants with foreign medical degrees (Weinar 2019). In many cases, even academic qualifications, such as PhDs, are required to go through the equivalency procedure.

The difference might be felt on the meso-level, where returning own national can be perceived by employers as a valuable catch, depending on the country the emigrant is returning from (Kuschminder 2014; Van Houte et al. 2015; Weinar 2002). Many countries of the world value the Anglo-Saxon education or the Western professional experience. However, this bias can change over time. The story of "sea turtles" in China is of particular interest here (Hao and Welch 2012; Hao et al. 2016). Hao and Welch (2012) discusses the changing political and social context of the return of highly skilled migrants to China over three decades. According to the authors, in the early days of the China's opening, a foreign degree was sufficient to ensure a position on the labour market. Thirty years later, these degrees had devalued because of the high supply of such returnees. Labour market in China had adopted discriminatory views of international graduates and also more understanding of a value of a degree from various institutions. This is why the employment opportunities follow strictly the assumed ranking of the foreign institution (see also Hao et al. 2016). This bias, both towards foreign institutions in general, and the ones considered as "top" in particular, resembles the "country labelling" trend. On another level, returnees are cut off from the native professional and social networks because of their prolonged stay abroad during the formative years. They are also social and culturally challenged. As authors note, many need to adjust their expectations and especially behaviour when seeking for jobs.

The issues experienced on the labour market are valid for most highly skilled immigrants worldwide. However, some groups received a special attention among scholars because of their particular positioning on the labour market and specific migration trajectories that reflect the tensions between privilege and vulnerability. We will discuss their cases in the remainder of this chapter.

3.2.2 From Segregation to Integration? Expatriates and Immigrants

Literature on migrant integration has long considered non-labour market integration issues faced by highly skilled migrants as not interesting. Scholars have started to look into the issue only in the last decade or so. The main reason for this slow onset of interest is the definitional conundrum that has permeated the field for decades, notably the binary opposition of "immigrant/migrant" as set against "expatriate".

The dominant subject of integration studies are immigrants, indirectly defined as coming from poorer countries to the industrialised countries. Ethnic and racial distinction is very much present in these deliberations. Social and cultural integration of diverse groups, where diversity is defined along religious or cultural denominators, is thus portrayed as a problem to be studied. This dominant approach in the field of migration studies has been juxtaposed by the niche studies of "expatriates," associated mostly as highly skilled white citizens of the developed countries, living in other (mostly developing) countries on a temporary basis. The notion of privilege has thus defined the mobility of what is perceived as a highly skilled global elite. For a long time, the privilege has been defined through the notions of citizenship, class and race (Kunz 2016) conflating the research on integration of highly skilled with the research on integration of "expatriates." In fact, highly-skilled migrants were identified as North-North migrants, characterised as "expatriates," "lifestyle migrants" (Benson and O'Reilly 2009), "cosmopolitans" (Brimm 2010), "Eurostars" (Favell 2011), as "elite migrants" (Beaverstock 2005), or "knowledge migrants" (Ackers 2005). They have been referred as "small, invisible, adaptable uncontroversial segment of migration (C. Knowles and Harper 2009, 7), i.e. people, who do not pose integration issues. Their migration process, from motivation to arrival has been described as different from the "standard" immigration (Favell 2011). The somewhat mythic idea that highly skilled migrants move because of motivations other than economic necessity and live in an undefined cosmopolitan sphere allows for a differentiation between immigrants and transnational knowledge workers (Colic-Peisker 2010), migrant professionals (Meyer 2011), or simply expatriates. Moreover, there is an assumption that while the first group is highly motivated to settle, the second one represents clearly "birds of passage" who do not want to go through the processes of incorporation and "acculturation". In other words, they were seen as an inconsequential object of study for integration literature and thus presented as non-immigrants. As such, they have been exempt from the expectation of integration, with, indeed, self-segregation seen as the norm (Beaverstock 2002; Cohen 1977; Croucher 2018; Fechter and Walsh 2010; Smith and Favell 2006). This self-segregation has not been seen as problematic as for example "ethnic enclave" or "ghettoization" phenomena observed among the non-highly-skilled or racialized immigrant population. For some scholars, this segregation, especially in the context of North-South mobility has been seen as a reproduction of the colonial patterns, with similar tendencies to live detached lives (Beaverstock 2002; Fechter and Walsh 2010; Leonard 2010, 2016).

Living in an "expat bubble," which was typical for an organisational expatriate might not be indeed an issue for a broader integration policy of a country (Findlay 1995; Fechter and Walsh 2010). The term itself has been used in a pejorative sense, like several other terms, e.g. "international jet set" (van Bochove and Engbersen 2015) suggesting that highly skilled immigrants tend to keep social networks mainly between themselves. And yet, this phenomenon should not be looked down upon as a revelation of some colonial prejudices: clearly, sharing migration journey with people who had similar experience of global mobility brings more security to the lives of these migrants, more psychological and emotional stability and thus integration to this milieu can be indeed effortless.

Yet, a closer look into the "expat bubble" shows a variety of ways the migrants themselves choose to approach their migration experience, which varies enormously, not only individually, but also across countries of destination and form of employment. Those who either are identified as expatriates or who call themselves expatriates – although many highly skilled Northerners reject that terminology (Klekowski von Koppenfels 2014) – belong to two groups of people: those who are organisational expatriates, and those who are highly skilled immigrants from Western developed countries. The fact of being called "an expatriate" has elevated them to an elite status in developing countries (Cohen 1977). Studies focusing on Dubai, for example, have shown that community of highly skilled immigrants from Western countries has developed a distinctive identity as different from other groups of immigrants, placed at the top of the migrant hierarchy (Coles and Walsh 2010; Fechter and Walsh 2010). The elite status had less to do with the expatriate status and related privileges (non-organisational expatriates enjoy none), but rather with the exogenous labels given by the society in the country of destination and defined by citizenship, race and class (Kunz 2016). In the same vein, Leonard (2010, 2016) suggests that the globalised labour market offers disparate rewards based on personal characteristics like 'race', gender and citizenship. As stated earlier, the "country labels" can be operationalized as the effects of the country of origin (Genova 2017). These labels are important prerequisites that support or challenge integration, but cannot be understood to be absolute across destination countries.

Given these labels, the Western skilled migrants in Dubai were defined in opposition to other migrants, regardless of skill level (Fechter and Walsh 2010). Leaving the expat bubble and refusing the label is virtually impossible in such environment. However, the dynamic of going out of the expat bubble has been observed in the case of organisational expatriates and highly skilled migrants living in less stringent contexts. Hence the emergence of the notion of the "middling migrant", not quite an expatriate and not quite a low-skilled migrant (Ho 2011; Luthra and Platt 2016; Maslova and Chiodelli 2018; Conradson and Latham 2005). The notion of "middling migrant" reflects the heterogeneity of the group and various life situations in which these individuals find themselves. Thanks to the new research in this area, the experiences of the highly skilled migrants from Western countries, who move for work across the globe, have been more nuanced. In fact, they have been more often regarded and studied as migrants. We know now that their experience differs from the experience of all other immigrants only to a certain extent. They integrate to varying degrees, and that depends on the context of reception, such as language spoken in the country (Klekowski von Koppenfels 2014; Dervin 2012; Föbker and Imani 2017).

The highly skilled also face stereotypes and bear the burden of acculturation processes (Weinar 2019), where the "expatriate" label often seems to be more of a liability than a help. Van Bochove and Engbersen (2015) demonstrated using the case of expatriates in Rotterdam that even expatriates' identifications are characterised by fragmentation, with a variety of integration outcomes in specific spheres of their lives: economic, political or social. The majority of their research subjects wished to be more integrated socially with the host society, but at the same time most of their close relationships were back in the countries of origin. This study brings thus to the forefront an important element, definitely understudied in the literature: the social cost of global mobility among the privileged groups. This raises interesting questions: we agree that low-skilled migrant moves out of necessity and the social cost involved in migration is taken for granted; why would then skilled privileged person moving out of choice agree to such a social cost (which remains the same in both cases). What is the calculation of costs and benefits in this case? We might then as well discover that economic necessity, measured against different criteria, lies at the heart of this decision. In some cases, as eloquently presented by Triandafyllidou and Isaakyan in their volume on 2008-crisis migration (Triandafyllidou and Isaakyan 2016), the economic necessity can be quite similar for all levels of skills, but the opportunities to migrate might not.

3.2.2.1 Highly Skilled Immigrants: Importance of a Place

The notion of locality in integration has been prevalent in the literature on integration of highly skilled migrants. The research done in this field has been driven mostly by sociologists and anthropologists, who have delivered many important ethnographic studies, almost exclusively focusing on integration as the relationship between the migrant and the locality in which they live. This place-based approach brings forward the interaction between the host and the foreigner on the micro-level of integration (Smith 2017; Bauder 2001; Meier 2014; Tseng 2011; Ryan and Mulholland 2014a). Comparison of the various cases creates a panoramic overview of how similar people live their integration in different localities. And because they do experience it differently, we might be prompted to ask why. The most striking difference comes with the treatment of the migrants from the Global North in different parts of the world.

As we have seen, many scholars would argue that the term expatriate is usually and intuitively reserved for 'Western' nationals who move abroad, that is to say, for (White) Western migrants. In contrast, citizens from less economically developed regions – who are not part of cosmopolitan elites – are typically termed immigrants or migrant workers (Yeoh and Willis 2005). This happens mostly in North-South migration contexts. As the literature on highly skilled migrant workers to Asia has shown, the "country label" can be the greatest liability. Camenisch and Suter (2019), for example have elaborated that being a Western, white foreign professional in a Chinese city is a double edged sword that not only provides the migrant with valuable human and cultural capital but at the same time restricts their economic activities to certain, albeit potentially lucrative, niches of the Chinese economy in which especially local hires and entrepreneurs face increasing competition by Chinese with similar levels of capital. Also, while European migrant professionals seem to benefit from an overall favourable image of western products and people when doing business or being employed in Chinese cities, not being a Chinese insider at the same time poses obstacles in terms of dealing with Chinese bureaucracy. They are also perceived as Others and not given the trust needed to build strong social relationships beyond the group of Westerners, which is usually a definition of failed integration. Similar issues have been found by Yeoh and Lam in their study of Singapore (Yeoh and Lam 2016) They found that discursive differentiation between "foreign talent" and the "Singaporean core" permeated the society and thus hurt integration efforts.

In the North-North context, to be discussed in the next chapter more in-depth, there is a growing number of non-organisational expatriates from Western countries, who see themselves as just immigrants (Klekowski von Koppenfels 2014; Weinar 2019). This admission reflects integration and adaptation processes that these people had to go through as immigrants to a country. This is especially the case with transatlantic migrations (see Chap. 4 for more in-depth analysis). The lives of Global Northerners in the Global North often hinge on "balancing acts" between local and transnational attachments (Erdal and Oeppen 2013; Dubucs et al. 2017). They can demonstrate what Triandafyllidou calls "plural nationalism," (Triandafyllidou 2013) as they cherish the attachment to several countries at the same time, which is easy to develop due to the facilitated mobility and communications between the countries (Ryan et al. 2015; Guitart and Mendoza 2008). Also, the Northerners in the North more often skip the kind of enclave settlements and living that is characteristic of communitarian forms of immigrant integration (Trenz and Triandafyllidou 2017; Plöger and Kubiak 2019; Dubucs et al. 2017). Scholars have been interested in the emergence of specific immigration hubs that seem to win the race for talent, mainly from the North (Jöns 2015; Ewers 2017). The emergence of such hubs, or Global Cities, is particularly well researched in the context of intra-European mobility. Highly skilled Europeans tend to move from various parts of

Europe to only a few countries, or even cities (Van Der Wende 2015). London has been a particularly well-researched migration hub, as it "offered opportunity for career escalation, enhanced remuneration, access to globally-connected social networks and onward mobility" (Ryan and Mulholland 2014c, p. 65). What differentiates these hubs from other places is the pull they have for highly-skilled migrants, which are often the result of economic and public policies: such as vibrant economy, multicultural appeal, quality of public services, or specific lifestyle (Beaverstock 2012; Tseng 2011; Ho 2011).

Highly-skilled migrants from the Global South in the Global North face often a different set of challenges (Lowell and Findlay 2001; Purkayastha 2005) that are closer to the experience of the low-skilled migrant than the idealized highly-skilled path to integration. Bauder (2001) describes the impact a cultural system in the country of origin can have on integration outcomes in Canada, arguing that there exists a certain hierarchy of migrants. In similar vein, Habti and Koikkalainen (2014) have analysed the migrant hierarchies in Finland, showing clearly that ethnicity and race play an important role in the integration dynamics. In both cases, the host society has different expectations and requirements towards different groups of migrants, placing those from the familiar cultures at the forefront.

The work on South-North migration has been developing quite fast, and within it a new strand of literature that looks at integration of highly-skilled migrants in the semi-periphery, notably post-communist countries of Central and Eastern Europe. The context of such integration is different: not post-colonial and not-quite-Western. Some work has been done on organisational expatriates, or corporate transferees, also under the label of "transnational elite" (Cook 2011; Piekut 2013), which depicts integration processes similar to those Westerners living in the Global South or places like Dubai. Only recently, a study by Bielewska (2018) brought to attention local integration challenges of a diverse group of highly skilled migrants (of the "middling" type) in one of the Polish cities (Wroclaw). She interviewed both white Europeans and an ethnically and racially diverse group of non-Europeans. She showed that all of them felt estranged in the country, but hold some links to the city they lived in. Those who found adaptation difficult were usually at odds with the local language, which they did not speak. Lack of language skills combined with the lack of English language skills among the population of Wroclaw made migrants feel uncomfortable and rejected. Migrants of different races or skin colour felt that they stand out from the population too homogenous to blend into, and they complained of being stared at. Most however have not reported any issues with practical sides of their integration, such as work with offices, or renting an apartment. Yet, their existence in Wroclaw is only in part reflective of the "middling migrant" experience. They tend to form an international enclave, a bubble of non-expatriates.

Highly skilled migrants have been largely thought to be easily adaptable, mostly because of the assumptions on their cultural background and "country labels". Their integration outcomes become even more difficult to grasp when we add gender to the mix.

3.2.2.2 From "Trailing Spouses" to Highly Skilled Migrants: Gender Dimension of Integration

Globally, perhaps contrary to expectation, more women than men migrate in the contemporary era. Among the highly-skilled, women are also over-represented (i.e. a larger share of skilled women migrate than skilled men) (OECD 2014; Docquier et al. 2009). However, they are often inactive or underemployed, as they often migrate as spouses or are employed as low skilled workers in the care sector, regardless of their training or education level (Kindler and Szulecka 2013; Marchetti and Venturini 2014). Within the highly skilled migration channels, women remain a minority and their presence in "organisational expatriate" flows has similarly also been a minority presence (Raghuram 2000; Vance and McNulty 2014). Indeed, they have been called "invisible" (Kofman 2000) as their presence is not captured by administrative statistics linked to the specific streams. Some countries, like Canada, have started to collect information on education levels and professional qualifications of dependants, but this information is lost when looking at women migrating through other streams (e.g. live-in care giver). All over the world, only women coming in through highly-skilled programs find their way to the statistics as highly skilled immigrants (Kofman and Raghuram 2015). The research into integration challenges of skilled women coming outside the highly skilled streams has been quite developed (Oso and Ribas-Mateos 2013; Triandafyllidou et al. 2016; Callister et al. 2006; Ryan 2019). In what follows, we focus on the questions of migration of women within the highly skilled streams; as dependants, and as the primary migrants.

Migrating Spouses
Migration of the highly skilled is rarely a lonely journey. International mobility of this group is, as it is for other migrant groups, also the mobility of a family. Arguably, temporary highly skilled migrants are more prone to transplant their families than e.g. temporary workers in agriculture, because the policy framework they migrate in allows for such moves. The effects of such moves for the family are felt by each of its members. The children who spend their childhoods moving from one country to another have even been dubbed "Third Culture Kids" (TCKs) (Pollock et al. 2010). Meanwhile, the spouses of the temporary highly-skilled migrants have been classified as "trailing spouses" recognizing that highly skilled migration is not necessarily a move undertaken as an employment-based migration project for both. The "trailing spouse" literature has shown that spouses of highly skilled immigrants are often highly skilled themselves, although many will not have a career. As an identifiable group of migrants, their integration pathways have been included as a research topic in the field.

There has been a rich literature on the "trailing spouse", usually conceptualised as a wife following her "organisational expatriate" or "corporate transferee" husband (Harvey 1998; Cooke 2001; Cangià 2018; Brandén et al. 2018). Only recently, in the view of the changing labour market dynamics and cultural acceptance, have we seen research on "trailing husbands" (Amcoff and Niedomysl 2015), both in opposite-sex and same-sex marriages (McPhail et al. 2016). Spouses in the "organisational expatriate" situation have been found to prioritise the careers of the employed partners and forego their own professional development. Researchers have found a strong tendency to engage in socialising lifestyles, focused on children, household and representation (Fechter 2010; Ryan and Mulholland 2014b; Beaverstock 2005). They are said to be at the core of the so-called expat bubble, as they build off-work relationships and networks within the "expatriate" communities. Van Bochove and Engbersen (2015), however, found strong fragmentation among the corporate transferees and their trailing spouses, with numerous patterns emerging, suggesting strong similarity to other migrants. Despite the increase in awareness of some dual career expatriate couples (McNulty and Moeller 2017), McNulty (2012) found that some spouses felt stigmatized by the "negative images" of the trailing spouse (cited in Collins and Bertone 2017, 86). Thanks to these stereotypes, the term "trailing spouse" has some negative overtones for their lived experience. Research into the experiences and adaptation of trailing spouses has found not only great variation in orientation toward different communities (van Bochove and Engbersen 2015), but also variation in adaptation, with many experiencing great difficulty, including identity crises (Collins and Bertone 2017). In some cases, their lack of adaptation leads to the spouse terminating a contract (Braseby 2010). Indeed, many spouses are found to not be satisfied with their lives (Kunz 2016; Fechter 2007; Yeoh and Khoo 1998), even if in a "golden cage" (Fechter 2007). As educated, highly skilled women raised in Western contemporary societies, they are aware of the open opportunity structures created for women as regards self-definition and control of their careers or their social status. They feel that there is an opportunity cost to their choice of living as a "trailing spouse," which affects their decision-making processes (Box 3.3).

Box 3.3: The Trailing Spouse

In an earlier era of more traditional roles, the trailing spouse was often a stay-at-home mother. In more recent years, however, new and varied patterns have begun emerging.

Increasingly, highly-skilled migration includes two working spouses, sometimes with one commuting. Other patterns include the wife as the primary worker, and the husband as the trailing spouse.

A more recently emerging pattern is that of the same-sex married couple, with one spouse the primary earner and the other the trailing spouse.

The rise of the male trailing spouse – whether heterosexual or homosexual – has revealed the gendered nature of the organisational expatriate social life, centred, for instance, around American Women's Clubs, which are present throughout the world. American Women's Clubs may well have a stronger representation of corporate expatriate trailing spouses, rather than a cross-section of overseas Americans, but this is, even so, a pertinent example of the gendered nature of available infrastructure.

The situation of non-employment of the highly-skilled spouses of "organisational expatriates" has been indeed at the core of some changes in the migration policies over the recent years. In Europe and in North America, spouses used to be automatically issued dependents' visas that would not give access to the labour market (Bauder 2005; Man 2004). The regulatory frameworks have evolved, especially for Intra-Corporate Transferees: under the EU ICT directive or under the Canadian framework (defined e.g. in the CETA), the spouses of skilled migrants moving within transnational companies have access to the local labour market and integration support. This is not, however, the case across the board.

Early research on family migration showed that women migrating as spouses, even if highly skilled, encounter substantial barriers to their career development (Iredale 2005; Aure 2013). The difficulties, as demonstrated here, are mainly created by the overall expectation that a migrating dependent woman would focus on raising a family and slowly improve her skills to match the needs of the labour market. Some scholars suggest that highly skilled migration policies reproduce and perpetuate archaic gender roles, with the men as principal bread winners and skilled workers and women as housewives focusing on the home. They do little to account for the changing reality of highly skilled families, where highly skilled men marry highly skilled women, where both partners have some career goals. For example, Bauder (2005), in his research on immigrants' integration in Greater Vancouver has found that spouses admitted to Canada for family reunion have less support in integration on the labour market than women who come as highly skilled immigrants in their own right. Weinar (2019) found the same challenges facing highly skilled spouses of European immigrants to Canada. Immigrant spouses would often subdue to the expectation that the career of the primary migrant should be stabilised before they start taking care of their own professional life. Research by Vergés Bosch and González Ramos (2013) has showed that migrating dependent highly skilled women, especially when they have children, are often victims of the family dynamics, where the men focus on their traditional roles, not supporting the career needs of their spouses. However, a supportive partner and the right feminist context can improve women's labour market integration. Yet, in the absence of those, there is an important brain waste among these women.

Highly Skilled Women as Primary Migrants
Highly skilled migrant women are one component of the highly skilled migration streams. They pursue their career or may follow a partner, but do not necessarily go through the family reunification channels. Their adaptation and integration processes are similar to that of their male counterparts, yet family and social expectations seem to shape their migratory experiences to a greater extent. Researchers who conduct research in this field often reflect on the social embeddedness of women and analyse their career development through the lens of their romantic ore sexual relationships (Isaakyan and Triandafyllidou 2014; D'Aoust 2013; Sinke 1999; Mai and King 2009). Van den Bergh and Plessis (2012) noted that migrating highly skilled women have strong agency, choosing to move their careers to another level, or even deciding to abandon them altogether, by migrating in a specific life

phase (see also Vance and McNulty 2014). They found that migration is less challenging for younger women (in their twenties), who are not yet established in their careers in their countries of origin and may find more opportunity to re-invent themselves abroad, while for older women the reinvention process concerns not only a career but also a social network, which is more difficult to establish later in life. It seems from this account that career and social embeddedness are equally important for these migrating women, and the absence of one of these components makes for a failed migration experience. In a similar vein, Dani Kranz, in her study of highly skilled foreign partners and spouses of Israeli citizens, finds that highly skilled women from the Global North experience two key difficulties in their lives: they experience not only professional status deprivation, but also social marginalization (Kranz 2019). In the Israeli case especially, the gendered and ethnicity-bound labour market is closed, she found, to the highly skilled foreign women. This closure is perpetuated by migration laws that exclude foreigners, but especially foreign women from gaining full legal participation in the society (citizenship rights). This legal shortcoming is then combined with the traditional views on the role of women in Israeli society, what can effectively extinguish all ambition on the part of the highly skilled female migrant.

Indeed, in many instances the labour markets do not send positive reinforcement towards highly skilled female migrants. As we noted above, the labour markets are skewed towards male participation and offer a clear gender and ethnic dividend to white males. Even if there is no racial difference (coming e.g. from the Global North), their gender has an adverse effect on their employability or career. This is especially true in some sectors of the economy, e.g. in STEM fields, as found by Grigoleit-Richter in Germany (2017). The process of "othering" in highly gender-segregated sectors combined with ethnic discrimination slows down the career development of white highly skilled women and effectively blocks career development of those coming from ethnic minorities (Richter). These findings are context-dependent, however. Other studies on women coming from more traditional societies in the Global South, show that migration can represent an opportunity to diverge from normative paths and escape from patriarchal norms, giving these women a possibility to engage more fully in professional lives (Kõu and Bailey 2017).

In all these instances, the social relations and networks built by the women in their host countries seem to be as important or even more important than the career itself, which corroborates the idea that women approach their professional international moves in a more complex manner and should be studied as such.

This duality of issues in the case of women is also present in the scarce literature on return of highly skilled women. The few studies that have been done show that return and reintegration is a family project in which the family members can be constraints or enablers of readjustment (Konzett-Smoliner 2016). The challenges to reintegration are quite important for non-native family members and for children raised abroad, and they include the usual challenges of integration: lacking language skills, inexistent social networks, difficulties with recognition of qualifications. Amcoff and Niedomysl (2015) provide an interesting insight on the effects of return on men accompanying women. They find that men are rarely gainer in this mobility, while women usually either experiences the greatest income increase by moving or compensate for the slighter economic gains with greater social and emotional gains.

Finally, we must underline that gender issues are not necessarily women's issues. However, little is known about other forms of gender experience in highly skilled migration. There has been some research done on the small number of cases where husbands accompany women in their international career moves or join them as spouses (Aure 2013; Cole 2012; Gallo 2006). Other aspects of gendered migration are still to be uncovered, including further research on same-sex couples. There remain areas for future research.

3.3   Conclusions

There has been substantial literature on specific patterns of integration among highly-skilled migrants (Nohl et al. 2014; Duchêne-Lacroix and Koukoutsaki-Monnier 2016; Ryan and Mulholland 2014a, b; King and Raghuram 2013; Piekut 2013; Fechter and Walsh 2010; Fechter 2007), but an examination of the integration of these migrants as migrants is still lacking, as van Bochove and Engbersen note: "studying them [corporate expatriates] as a type of migrants who experience partial inclusion and exclusion in their host society is a more fruitful approach" (2015, 307). Just as highly-skilled migrants are often portrayed as something other than migrants, their integration is similarly often portrayed as a phenomenon separate from that of lesser-skilled migrants. When discussing highly skilled migration, Smith and Favell (2006) argued that integration policy seems to be thought unnecessary for this category of migrants. Yet, integration is a challenge for all migrants, regardless of skill level. Indeed, highly-skilled migrants are still migrants and they face similar set of barriers to the labour market and obstacles in cultural integration. Also, the highly-skilled are the very group that most often experiences employment below their skill level, loss of status and painful adjustment trajectories, which also seem to be exacerbated by migrants' gender (Gauthier 2016; Adamuti-Trache 2011; Purkayastha 2005). Their migration trajectories and possible success are shaped by several factors that can be applied to any migration and have been discussed in literature: the way they enter a country (with a job offer or not); marketability of skills that they have (in IT sector or other sectors), existence of strong networks (Zikic et al. 2010; Mahroum 2000). In addition, highly-skilled often compete for jobs with the highly-skilled natives and that competition is more fierce than the one on the lower skill levels (Cantwell 2011; Schuster et al. 2013). The policy context is also crucial: intra-EU movers will face less hurdles to their integration than transatlantic movers. Also integration support in the host countries focuses on low-skilled immigration: highly-skilled are often left to their own devices to create a life on their own (Buzdugan and Halli 2009; She and Wotherspoon 2013). This often includes painful transitions for trailing spouses and children. Arguably, however, integration seems to be more difficult in the case of the South-North migration, because of the racial or cultural contexts they find themselves in. As some researchers attest, the same challenges are part and parcel of North-South migrants. They are usually inserted in a labour market but for those who live in an international bubble, any meaningful integration may be nearly impossible (Lauring and Selmer 2010), with negative consequences for themselves and their families. We will look closer into these issues when discussing a specific case of transatlantic migrations in the next chapter.

References

Ackers, L. (2005). Moving people and knowledge: Scientific mobility in the European Union. *International Migration, 43*(5), 99–131.

Acosta, D. (2018). *The national versus the foreigner in South America*. Cambridge: Cambridge University Press.

Acosta, D., & Freier, L. F. (2018). Regional governance of migration in South America. In *Handbook of migration and globalisation* (Vol. 69). Cheltenham: Edward Elgar Publishing.

Adamuti-Trache, M. (2011). First 4 years in Canada: Post-secondary education pathways of highly educated immigrants. *Journal of International Migration and Integration/Revue de l'integration et de La Migration Internationale, 12*(1), 61–83.

Agrawal, A., Kapur, D., McHale, J., & Oettl, A. (2011). Brain drain or brain bank? The impact of skilled emigration on poor-country innovation. *Journal of Urban Economics, 69*(1), 43–55.

Agunias, D. R. (2008). *Managing temporary migration: Lessons from the Philippine model*. Washington, DC: Migration Policy Institute.

Amcoff, J., & Niedomysl, T. (2015). Is the tied returnee male or female? The trailing spouse thesis reconsidered. *Population, Space and Place, 21*(8), 872–881.

Anisef, P., Sweet, R., & Frempong, G. (2003). Labour market outcomes of immigrant and racial minority university graduates in Canada. *Journal of International Migration and Integration/ Revue de l'integration et de La Migration Internationale, 4*(4), 499.

Arcarazo, D. A., & Geddes, A. (2014). Transnational diffusion or different models? Regional approaches to migration governance in the European Union and MERCOSUR. *European Journal of Migration and Law, 16*(1), 19–44.

Argote, L., & Ingram, P. (2000). Knowledge transfer: A basis for competitive advantage in firms. *Organizational Behavior and Human Decision Processes, 82*(1), 150–169.

Assirelli, G., Barone, C., & Recchi, E. (2019). You better move on': Determinants and labor market outcomes of graduate migration from Italy. *International Migration Review, 53*(1), 4–25. https://doi.org/10.1177/0197918318767930.

Aumüller, J. (2016). *Arbeitsmarktintegration von Flüchtlingen: Bestehende Praxisansätze Und Weiterführende Empfehlungen*. Gütersloh: Bertelsmann Stiftung.

Aure, M. (2013). Highly skilled dependent migrants entering the labour market: Gender and place in skill transfer. *Geoforum, 45*(March), 275–284.

Basran, G. S., & Zong, L. (1998). Devaluation of foreign credentials as perceived by visible minority professional immigrants.(1). *Canadian Ethnic Studies Journal, 30*(3), 6–26.

Basri, E., & Box, S. (Eds.). (2008). *The global competition for talent: Mobility of the highly skilled*. Paris: OECD.

Bauder, H. (2001). Culture in the labor market: Segmentation theory and perspectives of place. *Progress in Human Geography, 25*(1), 37–52.

Bauder, H. (2005). Habitus, rules of the labour market and employment strategies of immigrants in Vancouver, Canada. *Social & Cultural Geography, 6*(1), 81–97.

Beaverstock, J. V. (2002). Transnational elites in global cities: British expatriates in Singapore's financial district. *Geoforum, 33*(4), 525–538.

Beaverstock, J. V. (2005). Transnational elites in the city: British highly-skilled inter-company transferees in New York City's financial district. *Journal of Ethnic and Migration Studies, 31*(2), 245–268.

Beaverstock, J. V. (2012). Highly skilled international labour migration and world cities: Expatriates, executives and entrepreneurs. In *International handbook of globalization and world cities* (pp. 240–250). Cheltenham/Northhampton: Edward Elgar Publishing.

Beck, S., & Weinar, A. (2017). Mobile French citizens and La Mère-Patrie: Emigration and diaspora policies in France. In *Emigration and diaspora policies in the age of mobility* (pp. 85–99). Springer. https://link.springer.com/chapter/10.1007/978-3-319-56342-8_6

Beine, M., Docquier, F., & Rapoport, H. (2001). Brain drain and economic growth: Theory and evidence. *Journal of Development Economics, 64*(1), 275–289.

Benson, M., & O'Reilly, K. (2009). Migration and the search for a better way of life: A critical exploration of lifestyle migration. *The Sociological Review, 57*(4), 608–625.

Benson-Rea, M., & Rawlinson, S. (2003). Highly skilled and business migrants: Information processes and settlement outcomes. *International Migration, 41*(2), 59–79.

Bhagwati, J., & Rodriguez, C. (1975). Welfare-theoretical analyses of the brain drain. *Journal of Development Economics, 2*(3), 195–221.

Bielewska, A. (2018). Game of labels: Identification of highly skilled migrants. *Identities*, 1–19.

Blitz, B. K. (1999). Professional mobility and the mutual recognition of qualifications in the European Union: Two institutional approaches. *Comparative Education Review, 43*(3), 311–331.

Boeri, T., Brücker, H., Docquier, F., & Rapoport, H. (2012). *Brain drain and brain gain the global competition to attract high-skilled migrants.* Oxford: Oxford University Press.

Börzel, T. A., & Risse, T. (2012). From Europeanisation to diffusion: Introduction. *West European Politics, 35*(1), 1–19.

Bourdieu, P. (1986). The forms of capital. In J. G. Richardson (Ed.), *Handbook of theory and research for the sociology of education* (pp. 241–259). New York: Green Word Press.

Bourdieu, P. (2017). Habitus. In *Habitus: A sense of place* (pp. 59–66). London: Routledge.

Brandén, M., Bygren, M., & Gaehler, M. (2018). Can the trailing spouse phenomenon be explained by employer recruitment choices? *Population, Space and Place, 24*(6).

Braseby, A. M. (2010). *Adaptation of trailing spouses: Does gender matter?* ProQuest Dissertations Publishing.

Breschi, S., Lissoni, F., & Miguelez, E. (2017). Foreign-origin inventors in the USA: Testing for diaspora and brain gain effects. *Journal of Economic Geography, 17*(5), 1009–1038.

Brimm, L. (2010). *Global cosmopolitans: The creative edge of difference.* Springer.

Brzozowski, J. (2008). *Brain drain or brain gain? The new economics of brain drain reconsidered.* The New Economics of Brain Drain Reconsidered (October 22, 2008).

Buzdugan, R., & Halli, S. S. (2009). Labor market experiences of Canadian immigrants with focus on foreign education and experience. *International Migration Review, 43*(2), 366–386.

Callister, P., Bedford, R., Didham, R. A., & Statistics New Zealand. (2006). *Globalisation, gendered migration and labour markets.* Department of Labour.

Camenisch, A., & Suter, B. (2019). European migrant professionals in Chinese global cities: A diversified labour market integration. *International Migration, 57*(3), 208–221.

Cangià, F. (2018). Precarity, imagination, and the mobile life of the 'trailing spouse'. *Ethos, 46*(1), 8–26.

Cantwell, B. (2011). Transnational mobility and international academic employment: Gatekeeping in an academic competition arena. *Minerva, 49*(4), 425–445.

Castles, S., Miller, M. J., & de Haas, H. (1969. 2014). *The age of migration: International population movements in the modern world* (5th ed.). New York: Guilford Press.

Cerna, L. (2009). The varieties of high-skilled immigration policies: Coalitions and policy outputs in advanced industrial countries. *Journal of European Public Policy, 16*(1), 144–161.

Cerna, L. (2013a). The EU blue card: Preferences, policies, and negotiations between member states. *Migration Studies, 2*(1), 73–96.

Cerna, L. (2013b). Understanding the diversity of EU migration policy in practice: The implementation of the blue card initiative. *Policy Studies, 34*(2), 180–200.

Cerna, L. (2016). *Immigration policies and the global competition for talent*. Springer.

Cerna, L., & Czaika, M. (2016). European policies to attract talent: The crisis and highly skilled migration policy changes. In *High-skill migration and recession* (pp. 22–43). Springer.

Chiswick, B. R. (2011). *High-skilled immigration in a global labor market*. Washington, DC: AEI Press. http://www.aei.org/publication/high-skilled-immigration-in-a-global-labor-market/

Cohen, E. (1977). Expatriate communities. *Current Sociology, 24*(3), 5–90.

Cohen, N., & Kranz, D. (2015). State-assisted highly skilled return programmes, national identity and the risk (s) of homecoming: Israel and Germany compared. *Journal of Ethnic and Migration Studies, 41*(5), 795–812.

Cole, N. D. (2012). Expatriate accompanying partners: The males speak. *Asia Pacific Journal of Human Resources, 50*(3), 308–326.

Coles, A., & Walsh, K. (2010). From 'trucial state' to 'postcolonial' city? The imaginative geographies of British expatriates in Dubai. *Journal of Ethnic and Migration Studies, 36*(8), 1317–1333.

Colic-Peisker, V. A. L. (2010). Free floating in the cosmopolis? Exploring the identity-belonging of transnational knowledge workers. *Global Networks, 10*(4), 467–488.

Collins, H., & Bertone, S. (2017). Threatened identities: Adjustment narratives of expatriate spouses. *Journal of Global Mobility: The Home of Expatriate Management Research, 5*(1), 78–92.

Commander, S., Kangasniemi, M., & Alan Winters, L. (2004). The brain drain: Curse or boon? A survey of the literature. In *Challenges to globalization: Analyzing the economics* (pp. 235–278). Chicago: University of Chicago Press.

Conradson, D., & Latham, A. (2005). Transnational urbanism: Attending to everyday practices and Mobilities. *Journal of Ethnic and Migration Studies, 31*(2), 227–233. https://doi.org/10.108 0/1369183042000339891.

Cook, A. C. G. (2011). Placing capital (s): Everyday social transformations of transnational elites in Prague, Czech Republic. *Area, 43*(4), 420–429.

Cooke, T. J. (2001). 'Trailing wife' or 'Trailing mother'? The effect of parental status on the relationship between family migration and the labor-market participation of married women. *Environment and Planning A, 33*(3), 419–430.

Croucher, S. (2018). *Globalization and belonging: The politics of identity in a changing world*. Lanham: Rowman & Littlefield.

Currie, S. (2016). *Migration, work and citizenship in the enlarged European Union*. London/New York: Routledge.

Czaika, M. (2018). *High-skilled migration: Drivers and policies*. Oxford: Oxford University Press.

Czaika, M., & Parsons, C. R. (2017). The gravity of high-skilled migration policies. *Demography, 54*(2), 603–630.

D'Aoust, A.-M. (2013). In the name of Love: Marriage migration, governmentality, and technologies of love. *International Political Sociology, 7*(3), 258–274.

Davoudi, S., Wishardt, M., & Strange, I. (2010). The ageing of Europe: Demographic scenarios of Europe's futures. *Futures, 42*(8), 794–803.

De Haas, H. (2010). Migration and development: A theoretical perspective1. *International Migration Review, 44*(1), 227–264.

Dervin, F. (2012). Cultural identity, representation and othering. *The Routledge Handbook of Language and Intercultural Communication, 2*, 181–194.

Desiderio, M. V., & Weinar, A. (2014). *Supporting immigrant integration in Europe? Developing the governance for diaspora engagement*. Migrationpolicy.Org. May 2014. http://www.migrationpolicy.org/research/immigrant-integration-europe-developing-governance-diaspora-engagement

Docquier, F., & Marfouk, A. (2006). International migration by education attainment, 1990–2000. In *International migration, remittances and the brain drain* (pp. 151–199). Washington, DC: World Bank: Palgrave Macmillan.

Docquier, F., & Rapoport, H. (2012). Globalization, brain drain, and development. *Journal of Economic Literature, 50*(3), 681–730.

Docquier, F., Lindsay Lowell, B., & Marfouk, A. (2009). A gendered assessment of highly skilled emigration. *Population and Development Review, 35*(2), 297–321.

Doherty, N. (2013). Understanding the self-initiated expatriate: A review and directions for future research. *International Journal of Management Reviews, 15*(4), 447–469.

Dubucs, H., Pfirsch, T., Recchi, E., & Schmoll, C. (2017). Je Suis Un Italien de Paris: Italian migrants' incorporation in a European capital city. *Journal of Ethnic and Migration Studies, 43*(4), 578–595.

Duchêne-Lacroix, C., & Koukoutsaki-Monnier, A. (2016). Mapping the social space of transnational migrants on the basis of their (supra) national belongings: The case of French citizens in Berlin. *Identities, 23*(2), 136–154.

Erdal, M. B., & Oeppen, C. (2013). Migrant balancing acts: Understanding the interactions between integration and transnationalism. *Journal of Ethnic and Migration Studies, 39*(6), 867–884.

Erel, U. (2010). Migrating cultural capital: Bourdieu in migration studies. *Sociology, 44*(4), 642–660.

European Migration Network. (2013). *Attracting highly qualified and qualified third-country nationals*. EMN synthesis report. http://emn.ie/files/p_201311180323172013_attractinghq-workers_finalversion_23oct2013.pdf

Ewers, M. C. (2017). International knowledge mobility and urban development in rapidly globalizing areas: Building global hubs for talent in Dubai and Abu Dhabi. *Urban Geography, 38*(2), 291–314.

Fabry, N. H., & Zeghni, S. H. (2003). FDI in CEECs: How do western investors survive? *Thunderbird International Business Review, 45*(2), 133–147.

Facchini, G., & Lodigiani, E. (2014). Attracting skilled immigrants: An overview of recent policy developments in advanced countries. *National Institute Economic Review, 229*(1), R3–R21.

Faini, R. (2007). Remittances and the brain drain: Do more skilled migrants remit more? *The World Bank Economic Review, 21*(2), 177–191.

Favell, A. (2011). *Eurostars and Eurocities: Free movement and mobility in an integrating Europe* (Vol. 56). London: Wiley.

Fechter, A.-M. (2007). *Going first class?: New approaches to privileged travel and movement* (V. Amit, Ed.). New York: Berghahn Books.

Fechter, A.-M. (2010). Gender, empire, global capitalism: Colonial and corporate expatriate wives. *Journal of Ethnic and Migration Studies, 36*(8), 1279–1297. https://doi.org/10.1080/13691831003687717.

Fechter, A.-M., & Walsh, K. (2010). Examining 'expatriate' continuities: Postcolonial approaches to mobile professionals. *Journal of Ethnic and Migration Studies, 36*(8), 1197–1210. https://doi.org/10.1080/13691831003687667.

Felbermayr, G. J., & Toubal, F. (2012). Revisiting the trade-migration nexus: Evidence from new OECD data. *World Development, 40*(5), 928–937.

Findlay, A. (1995). Skilled transients? An invisible phenomenon? In *The Cambridge survey of world migration*. Cambridge: Cambridge University Press.

Flisi, S., & Murat, M. (2011). The hub continent. Immigrant networks, emigrant diasporas and FDI. *The Journal of Socio-Economics, 40*(6), 796–805.

Föbker, S., & Imani, D. (2017). The role of language skills in the settling-in process – Experiences of highly skilled migrants' accompanying partners in Germany and the UK. *Journal of Ethnic and Migration Studies, 43*(16), 2720. https://doi.org/10.1080/1369183X.2017.1314596.

Gallo, E. (2006). Italy is not a good place for men: Narratives of places, marriage and masculinity among Malayali migrants. *Global Networks, 6*(4), 357–372.

Gao, L., Liu, X., & Zou, H. (2013). The role of human mobility in promoting Chinese outward FDI: A neglected factor? *International Business Review, 22*(2), 437–449.

Gauthier, C.-A. (2016). Obstacles to socioeconomic integration of highly-skilled immigrant women: Lessons from Quebec interculturalism and implications for diversity management. *Equality, Diversity and Inclusion: An International Journal, 35*(1), 17–30.

Gawrich, A., Melnykovska, I., & Schweickert, R. (2010). Neighbourhood Europeanization through ENP: The case of Ukraine. *JCMS: Journal of Common Market Studies, 48*(5), 1209–1235.

Geddes, A. (2018). The politics of European Union migration governance: EU migration governance. *JCMS: Journal of Common Market Studies, 56*, 120–130.

Genova, E. (2017). 'Between a rock and a hard place': Bulgarian highly skilled migrants' experiences of external and internal stereotypes in the context of the European crisis. *National Identities, 19*(1), 33–51.

Ghosh, B. (2006). *Migrants' remittances and development: Myths, rhetoric and realities.* Geneva: International Organization for Migration.

Glaser, W. A., & Christopher Habers, G. (1978). *The brain drain: Emigration and return: Findings of a UNITAR multinational comparative survey of professional personnel of developing countries who study abroad.* Oxford/New York: Pergamon Press.

Grant, H., & Sweetman, A. (2004). Introduction to economic and urban issues in Canadian immigration policy. *Canadian Journal of Urban Research, 13*(1), 1–24.

Green, A. G., & Green, D. A. (1995). Canadian immigration policy: The effectiveness of the point system and other instruments. *Canadian Journal of Economics, 28*(4), 1006–1041.

Grigoleit-Richter, G. (2017). Highly skilled and highly mobile? Examining gendered and ethnicised labour market conditions for migrant women in STEM-professions in Germany. *Journal of Ethnic and Migration Studies, 43*(16), 2738.

Guitart, A. O., & Mendoza, C. (2008). Vivir (En) La Ciudad de México: Espacio Vivido e Imaginarios Espaciales de Un Grupo de Migrantes de Alta Calificación. *Latin American Research Review, 43*(1), 113–138.

Habti, D., & Koikkalainen, S. (2014). *International highly skilled migration: The case of Finland.* Huntsville: Journal of Finnish Studies.

Hao, J., & Welch, A. (2012). A tale of sea turtles: Job-seeking experiences of Hai Gui (High-Skilled Returnees) in China. *Higher Education Policy, 25*(2), 243–260.

Hao, J., Wen, W., & Welch, A. (2016). When sojourners return: Employment opportunities and challenges facing high-skilled Chinese returnees. *Asian and Pacific Migration Journal, 25*(1), 22–40.

Harvey, M. (1998). Dual-career couples during international relocation: The trailing spouse. *The International Journal of Human Resource Management, 9*(2), 309.

Harvey, W. (2012). Brain circulation to the UK? Knowledge and investment flows from highly skilled British expatriates in Vancouver. *Journal of Management Development, 31*(2), 173–186.

Hercog, M., & Sandoz, L. (2018). Highly skilled or highly wanted migrants? Conceptualizations, policy designs and implementations of high-skilled migration policies. *Migration Letters, 15*(4), 453–460. https://doi.org/10.33182/ml.v15i4.534.

Hercog, M., & Siegel, M. (2011). *Promoting return and circular migration of the highly skilled* (SSRN Scholarly Paper ID 1949705). Rochester: Social Science Research Network. https://papers.ssrn.com/abstract=1949705.

Ho, E. L.-E. (2011). Migration trajectories of 'highly skilled' middling transnationals: Singaporean transmigrants in London. *Population, Space and Place, 17*(1), 116–129.

Hoff, A. (2011). *Population ageing in Central and Eastern Europe: Societal and policy implications.* Farnham/Burlington: Ashgate Publishing.

Iredale, R. (2000). Migration policies for the highly skilled in the Asia-Pacific region. *International Migration Review, 34*(3), 882–906.

Iredale, R. (2005). Gender, immigration policies and accreditation: Valuing the skills of professional women migrants. *Geoforum, 36*(2), 155–166.

Isaakyan, I., & Triandafyllidou, A. (2014). Anglophone marriage-migrants in Southern Europe: A study of expat nationalism and integration dynamics. *International Review of Sociology, 24*(3), 374–390.

Jöns, H. (2009). 'Brain circulation' and transnational knowledge networks: Studying long-term effects of academic mobility to Germany, 1954–2000. *Global Networks, 9*(3), 315–338.

Jöns, H. (2015). Talent mobility and the shifting geographies of Latourian knowledge hubs. *Population, Space and Place, 21*(4), 372–389.

Jurgens, J. (2010). The legacies of labor recruitment: The guest worker and green card programs in the Federal Republic of Germany. *Policy and Society, 29*(4), 345–355.

Kaczmarczyk, P., Lesinska, M., Warszawski, U., & Osrodek Badan nad Migracjami. (2012). *Krajobrazy migracyjne Polski*. Warszawa: Osrodek Badan nad Migracjami Uniwersytetu Warszawskiego.

Kapur, D., & McHale, J. (2005a). *Give us your best and brightest: The global hunt for talent and its impact on the developing world*. Washington, DC: Center for Global Development.

Kapur, D., & McHale, J. (2005b). Mobile human capital and high-tech industry development in India, Ireland, and Israel. In *From underdogs to tigers: The rise and growth of the software industry in Brazil, China, India, Ireland, and Israel* (Vol. 236). Oxford: Oxford University Press.

Kaur, A. (2018). Patterns and governance of labour migration in ASEAN: Regional policies and migration corridors. In *Handbook of migration and globalisation* (p. 105). Cheltenham: Edward Elgar Publishing.

Kerr, S. P., Kerr, W., Ozden, C., & Parsons, C. (2016). *Global talent flows*. Washington, DC: The World Bank.

Kindler, M., & Szulecka, M. (2013). The economic integration of Ukrainian and Vietnamese migrant women in the Polish labour market. *Journal of Ethnic and Migration Studies, 39*(4), 649–671.

King, R., & Raghuram, P. (2013). International student migration: Mapping the field and new research agendas. *Population, Space and Place, 19*(2), 127–137.

Klagge, B., & Klein-Hitpass, K. (2010). High-skilled return migration and knowledge-based development in Poland. *European Planning Studies, 18*(10), 1631–1651.

Klekowski von Koppenfels, A. (2014). *Migrants or expatriates?: Americans in Europe*. Springer.

Kloc-Nowak, Weronika. (2013). *Highly skilled Indian migrants in Poland*.

Knowles, V. (2016). *Strangers at our gates: Canadian immigration and immigration policy, 1540–2015*. Toronto: Dundurn.

Knowles, C., & Harper, D. (2009). *Hong Kong: Migrant lives, landscapes, and journeys*. Chicago: University of Chicago Press.

Kofman, E. (2000). The invisibility of skilled female migrants and gender relations in studies of skilled migration in Europe. *International Journal of Population Geography, 6*(1), 45–59.

Kofman, E., & Raghuram, P. (2015). *Gendered migrations and global social reproduction*. Springer.

Koh, S. Y. (2015). State-led talent return migration programme and the doubly neglected 'Malaysian diaspora': Whose diaspora, what citizenship, whose development? *Singapore Journal of Tropical Geography, 36*(2), 183–200.

Kolbe, M., & Kayran, E. N. (2019, February). The limits of skill-selective immigration policies: Welfare states and the commodification of labour immigrants. *Journal of European Social Policy, 29*(4), 478–497.

Konzett-Smoliner, S. (2016). Return migration as a 'family project': Exploring the relationship between family life and the readjustment experiences of highly skilled Austrians. *Journal of Ethnic and Migration Studies, 42*(7), 1094–1114.

Koser, K., & Kuschminder, K. (2015). Comparative research on the assisted voluntary return and reintegration of migrants. In *International organization for migration*. Geneva: IOM Publications.

Koslowski, R. (2014). Selective migration policy models and changing realities of implementation. *International Migration, 52*(3), 26–39.

Kõu, A., & Bailey, A. (2017). 'Some people expect women should always be dependent': Indian women's experiences as highly skilled migrants. *Geoforum, 85*, 178–186.

Kranz, D. (2019). The Global North goes to the Global North minus? Intersections of the integration of highly skilled, non-Jewish female partner and spousal migrants from the Global North in Israel. *International Migration, 57*(3), 192–207.

Kugler, M., & Rapoport, H. (2005). *Skilled emigration, business networks and foreign direct investment*. https://papers.ssrn.com/sol3/papers.cfm?abstract_id=710923

Kumar, N. (2013). Internationalisation of Indian knowledge-intensive service firms: Learning as an antecedent to entrepreneurial orientation. *Asian Business & Management, 12*(5), 503–523.

Kunz, S. (2016). Privileged mobilities: Locating the expatriate in migration scholarship. *Geography Compass, 10*(3), 89–101.

Kuschminder, K. (2014). *Female return migration and reintegration strategies in Ethiopia*. PhD thesis, Maastricht University.

Lauring, J., & Selmer, J. (2010). The supportive expatriate spouse: An ethnographic study of spouse involvement in expatriate careers. *International Business Review, 19*(1), 59–69.

Lavenex, S. (2007). The competition state and highly skilled migration. *Society, 44*(2), 32.

Lazarowicz, A. (2013). *The intra-corporate transferees directive: Time to break the deadlock*. Brussels: European Policy Centre.

Leonard, P. (2010). Work, identity and change? Post/colonial encounters in Hong Kong. *Journal of Ethnic and Migration Studies, 36*(8), 1247–1263.

Leonard, P. (2016). *Expatriate identities in postcolonial organizations: Working whiteness*. London: Routledge.

Li, P. (2003). *Destination Canada: Immigration debates and issues*. Don Mills, Ontario: Oxford University Press.

Li, Q., & Sweetman, A. (2014). The quality of immigrant source country educational outcomes: Do they matter in the receiving country? *Labour Economics, 26*, 81–93.

Lodge, M. (2006). *The Europeanisation of governance-top down, bottom up or both?* Nomos Publishers. http://eprints.lse.ac.uk/26540.

Lowell, B. L., & Findlay, A. (2001). Migration of highly skilled persons from developing countries: Impact and policy responses. *International Migration Papers, 44*, 25.

Lucas, R. E. (2005). *International migration and economic development: Lessons from low-income countries*. Cheltenham: Edward Elgar Publishing.

Luthra, R., & Platt, L. (2016). Elite or middling? International students and migrant diversification. *Ethnicities, 16*(2), 316–344.

Mahroum, S. (2000). Highly skilled globetrotters: Mapping the international migration of human capital. *R&D Management, 30*(1), 23–32. https://doi.org/10.1111/1467-9310.00154.

Mai, N., & King, R. (2009). Love, sexuality and migration: Mapping the issue (s). *Mobilities, 4*(3), 295–307.

Man, G. (2004). Gender, work and migration: Deskilling Chinese immigrant women in Canada. In *Women's studies international forum* (Vol. 27, pp. 135–148). Elsevier.

Marchetti, S., & Venturini, A. (2014). Mothers and grandmothers on the move: Labour mobility and the household strategies of Moldovan and Ukrainian migrant women in Italy. *International Migration, 52*(5), 111–126.

Maslova, S., & Chiodelli, F. (2018). Expatriates and the city: The spatialities of the high-skilled migrants' transnational living in Moscow. *Geoforum, 97*(December), 209–218.

Mattoo, A., Neagu, I. C., & Ozden, C. (2005). *Brain waste? Educated immigrants in the US labor Market*. Washington, DC: The World Bank.

McLaughlan, G., & Salt, J. (2002). *Migration policies towards highly skilled foreign workers*. London: Home Office.

McNulty, Y. (2012). 'Being dumped in to sink or swim': An empirical study of organizational support for the trailing spouse. *Human Resource Development International, 15*(4), 417–434.

McNulty, Y., & Moeller, M. (2017). A typology of dual-career expatriate (trailing) spouses: The 'R' profile. In M. Dickmann, V. Suutari, & O. Wurtz (Eds.), *The management of global careers: Exploring the rise of international work*. London: Palgrave-Macmillan. (Forthcoming).

McPhail, R., McNulty, Y., & Hutchings, K. (2016). Lesbian and gay expatriation: Opportunities, barriers and challenges for global mobility. *The International Journal of Human Resource Management, 27*(3), 382–406.

Meier, L. (2014). *Migrant professionals in the city: Local encounters, Identities and Inequalities*. New York: Routledge.

Meyer, J.-B. (2011). A sociology of diaspora knowledge networks. In *The migration-development Nexus* (pp. 159–181). Springer.

Mountford, A. (1997). Can a brain drain be good for growth in the source economy? *Journal of Development Economics, 53*(2), 287–303.

Nohl, A.-M., Schittenhelm, K., Schmidtke, O., & Weiß, A. (2014). *Work in transition: Cultural capital and highly skilled migrants' passages into the labour market.* University of Toronto Press.

Nowicka, M. (2014). Migrating skills, skilled migrants and migration skills: The influence of contexts on the validation of migrants' skills. *Migration Letters, 11*(2), 171–186.

OECD. (2014). *Harnessing knowledge on the migration of highly skilled women – Overview of key findings.* Washington, DC: OECD, OECD Publications Center.

OECD, The World Bank, & International Organization for Migration. (2004). *Trade and migration: Building bridges for global labour mobility.* Paris: OECD.

Ojo, T. H., & Shizha, E. (2018). Ethnic enclaves in Canada: Opportunities and challenges of residing within. In E. Shizha, R. Kimani-Dupuis, & P. Broni (Eds.), *Living beyond borders: Essays on global immigrants and refugees* (pp. 162–179). New York: Peter Lang.

Oso, L., & Ribas-Mateos, N. (2013). *The international handbook on gender, migration and transnationalism.* Cheltenham: Edward Elgar Publishing.

Paul, R. (2016). Negotiating varieties of capitalism? Crisis and change in contemporary British and German labour migration policies. *Journal of Ethnic and Migration Studies, 42*(10), 1631–1650.

Picot, W. G., & Sweetman, A. (2004). *The deteriorating economic welfare of immigrants and possible causes.* Statistics Canada, Business and Labour Market Analysis Division.

Piekut, A. (2013). 'You've got starbucks and coffee heaven … i can do this!'spaces of social adaptation of highly skilled migrants in Warsaw. *Central and Eastern European Migration Review, 2*(1), 117–138.

Piore, M. J. (1970). *The dual labor market: Theory and implications.*

Pires, A. J. G. (2015). Brain drain and brain waste. *Journal of Economic Development, 40*(1), 1–34.

Plöger, J., & Kubiak, S. (2019). Becoming 'the internationals'—How place shapes the sense of belonging and group formation of high-skilled migrants. *Journal of International Migration and Integration, 20*(1), 307–321.

Pollock, D. C., Van Reken, R. E., & Pollock, M. V. (2010). *Third culture kids: The experience of growing up among worlds: The original, classic book on TCKs.* Hachette UK.

Portes, A., & Celaya, A. (2013). Modernization for emigration: Determinants & consequences of the brain drain. *DAEDALUS, 142*(3), 170–184.

Purkayastha, B. (2005). Skilled migration and cumulative disadvantage: The case of highly qualified Asian Indian immigrant Women in the US. *Geoforum, 36*(2), 181–196.

Raghuram, P. (2000). Gendering skilled migratory streams: Implications for conceptualizations of migration. *Asian and Pacific Migration Journal, 9*(4), 429–457.

Ratha, D. (2005). *Workers' remittances: An important and stable source of external development finance.* http://repository.stcloudstate.edu/cgi/viewcontent.cgi?article=1009&context=econ_seminars.

Rogers, R. (1997). *Migration return policies and the countries of origin.* Hailbronner, Kay; Martin, David; Motomura, Hiroshi.

Ryan, L. (2019). Narratives of settling in contexts of mobility: A comparative analysis of Irish and polish highly qualified women migrants in London. *International Migration, 57*(3), 177–191.

Ryan, L., & Mulholland, J. (2014a). Trading places: French highly skilled migrants negotiating mobility and emplacement in London. *Journal of Ethnic and Migration Studies, 40*(4), 584–600.

Ryan, L., & Mulholland, J. (2014b). 'Wives are the route to social life': An analysis of family life and networking amongst highly skilled migrants in London. *Sociology, 48*(2), 251–267.

Ryan, L., & Mulholland, J. (2014c). Doing the business: Variegation, opportunity and intercultural experience among intra- EU highly-skilled migrants. *International Migration, 52*(3), 55–68.

Ryan, L., von Koppenfels, A. K., & Mulholland, J. (2015). 'The distance between us': A comparative examination of the technical, spatial and temporal dimensions of the transnational social relationships of highly skilled migrants. *Global Networks, 15*(2), 198–216.

Sadowski-Smith, C., & Li, W. (2016). Return migration and the profiling of non-citizens: Highly skilled BRIC migrants in the Mexico–US Borderlands and Arizona's SB 1070. *Population, Space and Place, 22*(5), 487–500.

Salt, J., & Millar, J. (2006). International migration in interesting times: The case of the UK. *People and Place, 14*(2), 14.

Sardana, D., Zhu, Y., & Veen, R. (2016). Unlocking the talents-in-waiting: Case study analysis of Chinese and Indian high-skilled migrants in South Australia. *International Migration, 54*(6), 74–93.

Saxenian, A. L. (2005). From brain drain to brain circulation: Transnational communities and regional upgrading in India and China. *Studies in Comparative International Development, 40*(2), 35–61.

Schaafsma, J., & Sweetman, A. (2001). Immigrant earnings: Age at immigration matters. *Canadian Journal of Economics, 34*(4), 1066–1099.

Schiff, M. (2005). *Brain gain: Claims about its size and impact on welfare and growth are greatly exaggerated*. Washington, DC: The World Bank.

Schittenhelm, K., & Schmidtke, O. (2011). Integrating highly skilled migrants into the economy: Transatlantic perspectives. *International Journal, 66*(1), 127–143.

Schüller, S. (2016). *Ethnic enclaves and immigrant economic integration*. Bonn: IZA World of Labor.

Schuster, A., Vincenza Desiderio, M., & Urso, G. (2013). *Recognition of qualifications and competences of migrants*. Brussels: International Organization for Migration.

She, Q., & Wotherspoon, T. (2013). International student mobility and highly skilled migration: A comparative study of Canada, the United States, and the United Kingdom. *Springer Plus, 2*(1), 132.

Shima, I. (2010). *Return migration and labour market outcomes of the returnees. Does the return really pay off? The case-study of Romania and Bulgaria*. FIW Research Reports.

Siddiqui, Z., & Tejada, G. (2014). Development and highly skilled migrants: Perspectives from the Indian diaspora and returnees. *International Development Policy|Revue Internationale de Politique de Développement, 5*(5.2).

Sinatti, G. (2015). Return migration as a win-win-win scenario? Visions of return among Senegalese migrants, the state of origin and receiving countries. *Ethnic and Racial Studies, 38*(2), 275–291.

Sinke, S. (1999). Migration for labor, migration for love: Marriage and family formation across borders. *OAH Magazine of History, 14*(1), 17–21.

Slade, B., Luo, Y., & Schugurensky, D. (2005). Seeking 'Canadian experience': The informal learning of new immigrants as volunteer workers. In *24th annual conference of CASAE, London, Ontario*.

Smith, M. P. (2017, September 8). Transnational ties: Cities, migrations, and identities. *Transnational Ties*.

Smith, M. P., & Favell, A. (2006). *The human face of global mobility: International highly skilled migration in Europe, North America and The Asia-Pacific* (Vol. 8). Transaction Publishers.

Solimano, A. (2008). The international mobility of talent and economic development: An overview of selected issues. In *The international mobility of talent: Types causes and development impact* (pp. 21–43). Oxford: Oxford University Press.

Somerville, K. (2015). Strategic migrant network building and information sharing: Understanding 'migrant pioneers' in Canada. *International Migration, 53*(4), 135–154.

Somerville, K., & Walsworth, S. (2009). Vulnerabilities of highly skilled immigrants in Canada and the United States. *American Review of Canadian Studies, 39*(2), 147–161.

Stark, O., & Simon Fan, C. (2007). *Losses and gains to developing countries from the migration of educated workers: An overview of recent research, and new reflections*. ZEF Discussion Papers on Development Policy.

Stark, O., Helmenstein, C., & Prskawetz, A. (1997). A brain gain with a brain drain. *Economics Letters, 55*(2), 227–234.

Sumption, M. (2013). *Tackling brain waste: Strategies to improve the recognition of immigrants' foreign qualifications*. Washington, DC: Migration Policy Institute.

Sweetman, A. (2004). *Immigrant source country educational quality and Canadian labour market outcomes*. Analytical Studies, Statistics Canada.

Syed, J. (2008). Employment prospects for skilled migrants: A relational perspective. *Human Resource Management Review, 18*(1), 28–45.

Thondhlana, J., Madziva, R., & McGrath, S. (2016). Negotiating employability: Migrant capitals and networking strategies for Zimbabwean highly skilled migrants in the UK. *The Sociological Review, 64*(3), 575–592.

Tilly, C. (2007). Trust networks in transnational migration. In *Sociological forum* (Vol. 22, pp. 3–24). Wiley Online Library.

Trenz, H.-J., & Triandafyllidou, A. (2017). Complex and dynamic integration processes in Europe: Intra EU mobility and international migration in times of recession. *Journal of Ethnic and Migration Studies, 43*(4), 546–559.

Triandafyllidou, A. (2013). National identity and diversity: Towards plural nationalism. In *Tolerance, intolerance and respect* (pp. 159–185). Springer.

Triandafyllidou, A., & Isaakyan, I. (Eds.). (2016). European policies to attract talent: The crisis and highly skilled migration policy changes. In *High-skill migration and recession. migration, diasporas and citizenship*. London: Palgrave Macmillan.

Triandafyllidou, A., Isaakyan, I., & Schiavone, G. (2016). *High skill migration and recession: gendered perspectives*. Berlin: Springer.

Tseng, Y.-F. (2011). Shanghai rush: Skilled migrants in a fantasy city. *Journal of Ethnic and Migration Studies, 37*(5), 765–784.

Tung, R. L. (2008). Brain circulation, diaspora, and international competitiveness. *European Management Journal, 26*(5), 298–304.

van Bochove, M., & Engbersen, G. (2015). Beyond cosmopolitanism and expat bubbles: Challenging dominant representations of knowledge workers and trailing spouses. *Population Space and Place, 21*(4), 295–309.

van den Bergh, R., & Du Plessis, Y. (2012). Highly skilled migrant women: A career development framework. *The Journal of Management Development, 31*(2), 142.

Van Der Wende, M. (2015). International academic mobility: Towards a concentration of the minds in Europe. *European Review, 23*(S1), S70–S88.

Van Houte, M., & Davids, T. (2008). Development and return migration: From policy panacea to migrant perspective sustainability. *Third World Quarterly, 29*(7), 1411–1429.

Van Houte, M., Siegel, M., & Davids, T. (2015). Return to Afghanistan: Migration as reinforcement of socio-economic stratification. *Population, Space and Place, 21*(8), 692–703.

Vance, C. M., & McNulty, Y. (2014). Why and how women and men acquire global career experience: A study of American expatriates in Europe. *International Studies of Management & Organization, 44*(2), 34–54.

Vergés Bosch, N., & González Ramos, A. M. (2013). Beyond the work-life balance: Family and international mobility of the highly skilled. *Sociología y tecnociencia: Revista digital de sociología del sistema tecnocientífico, 3*, 55–76.

Weinar, A. (2002). Reemigranci Jako Aktorzy Zmiany Społecznej. In *Migracje Powrotne Polaków: Powroty Sukcesu Czy Rozczarowania* (pp. 39–78). Warszawa: Instytut Polityki Społecznej.

Weinar, A. (2010). Instrumentalising diasporas for development: International and European policy discourses. In *Diaspora and transnationalism: Concepts, theories and methods, edited by Faist Thomas and Rainer Baubock* (pp. 73–89). Amsterdam University Press.

Weinar, A. (Ed.). (2017a). *Emigration and diaspora policies in the age of mobility*. Cham: Springer.

Weinar, A. (2017b). From emigrants to free movers: Whither European emigration and diaspora policy? *Journal of Ethnic and Migration Studies, 43*(13), 1–19.

Weinar, A. (2019). *European citizenship and identity outside of the European Union*. London/New York: Routledge.

Werner, H. (2002). The current'green card'initiative for foreign IT specialists in Germany. In *International mobility of the highly skilled* (p. 321). Paris: OECD.

Wickramasekara, P. (2003). *Policy responses to skilled migration: Retention, return and circulation*. Geneva: International Labour Organization.

Wiesbrock, A., & Hercog, M. (2012). *Making Europe more attractive to Indian highly-skilled migrants. The blue card directive and national law in Germany and the Netherlands*. CARIM-India Research Report, 9.

Williams, A., & Baláž, V. (2014). *International migration and knowledge*. London: Routledge.

Wright, C. F. (2015). Why do states adopt liberal immigration policies? The policymaking dynamics of skilled visa reform in Australia. *Journal of Ethnic and Migration Studies, 41*(2), 306–328.

Wright, C. F., Clibborn, S., Piper, N., & Cini, N. (2016). *Economic migration and Australia in the 21st century*. Sydney: Lowy Institute for International Policy.

Yeoh, B. S. A., & Khoo, L.-M. (1998). Home, work and community: Skilled international migration and expatriate women in Singapore. *International Migration, 36*(2), 159–186.

Yeoh, B. S. A., & Lam, T. (2016). Immigration and its (Dis) contents: The challenges of highly skilled migration in globalizing Singapore. *American Behavioral Scientist, 60*(5–6), 637–658.

Yeoh, B. S. A., & Willis, K. (2005). Singaporean and British transmigrants in China and the cultural politics of 'contact zones'. *Journal of Ethnic and Migration Studies, 31*(2), 269–285.

Yost, E. G. (1996). NAFTA–temporary entry provisions–immigration dimensions. *Can.-USLJ, 22*, 211.

Zahlan, A. B. (1981). *The problematic of the Arab Brain drain* (pp. 9–10). London: The Arab Brain Drain, Ithaca Press.

Zikic, J., Bonache, J., & Cerdin, J.-L. (2010). Crossing national boundaries: A typology of qualified immigrants' career orientations. *Journal of Organizational Behavior, 31*(5), 667–686.

Chapter 4
Highly-Skilled Migrants in the Transatlantic Space: Between Settlement and Mobility

4.1 Transatlantic Migration System – A Case Study

In this chapter we look deeper into the specific case of Global Northerners who migrate within the Global North. Their case is used as an illustration of the complexities of highly skilled migration; these complexities impact lives of even the seemingly privileged mobile skilled people moving within the trans-Atlantic space of freer movement. At the heart of our discussion is an examination of the tension between settlement and mobility. On one hand, transatlantic migrants might have an easier time migrating than do Global Southerners because of specific privileged policy channels; on the other hand, they might also find it difficult to settle and they may return. Patterns of settlement and mobility are thus related to integration challenges which define North-North migration as much as any other migration. In our view, this case can serve as a broader generalisation about the experience of the highly skilled migrants (Box 4.1).

© The Author(s) 2020
A. Weinar, A. Klekowski von Koppenfels, *Highly-Skilled Migration: Between Settlement and Mobility*, IMISCOE Research Series,
https://doi.org/10.1007/978-3-030-42204-2_4

> **Box 4.1: Expats no More?**
> Recent research has moved beyond studying highly skilled migrants solely as a particular group of "expatriates" coming from the Global North, forming a sort of a "global super-class" or "transnational elite" of "self-initiated global careerists" (Ho 2011; Brimm 2010). While there certainly are migrants who fall into this category of very highly remunerated global elite migrants, we take a more critical stance towards this particular group here, noting that this group is becoming proportionally smaller than all other groups of highly skilled migrants, many of whom come instead from the global middle class (Conradson and Latham 2005; Ball and Nikita 2014; Rutten and Verstappen 2014). These highly-skilled migrants might just not be "masters of the free movement" (Smith and Favell 2006), as they were once called; they do not necessarily enjoy unprecedented liberty, mobility and recognition, even when compared to low-skilled migrants. They also have more to lose in terms of three forms of Bourdieu's capital. They are, literature increasingly seems to suggest, not as different from low-skilled migrants as they once were seen; rather, their gender, ethnicity, education, country of origin and migration destination may well play a stronger role in defining their migration trajectory and outcomes (Meier 2014).

To present our case study, we offer a general picture of highly skilled mobility over the Atlantic, then discuss mobility and integration drivers that influence this migration; and finally we discuss the integration outcomes of this particular group of migrants and the impact this migration has on the countries of origin and destination. Since it is North-North migration we go beyond the "migration and development" discourse, shedding the light on the challenges of economic measurement in the intertwined economies.

4.2   Emerging Patterns of Mobility: The Case of Transatlantic Migrations in Twenty-First Century

Migration studies today is largely based on an academic analysis of the transatlantic migration flows in the nineteenth and early twentieth centuries. The nascent field documented the arrival and settlement of millions of people from all over Europe, with various skill levels, making North America their home. Despite such publications as Mabogunje's 1970 system theory of migration, which also addressed skilled migration, with a focus on Africa, as well, the image of the immigrant as a permanent settler has defined perceptions of international migration well into the twenty-first century. Some research suggests that this image of the one-way, permanent immigration flow may be at least partially mythical with far higher rates of return that generally thought (Gabaccia 2013; Portes et al. 2003: 1215; Klekowski von Koppenfels 2014). Regardless of the extent to which the image of the permanent one-way migration from Europe to North America was reality or myth, these dynamics do change and, indeed, these changes are most visible in what is perhaps the longest studied migration system in the world.

The transatlantic migration system of today, at the beginning of the twenty-first century, does not resemble the system we knew 100 years ago. It is characterized by three main dynamics: decrease of migration flows and increase of short-term mobility; an increase of the average skill level of a migrant; and the rise of bi-directional migration and mobility.[1]

Of the immigrants to the US and Canada, the number of those who originate from Europe continues to shrink.[2] This is the sign not only of the growing numbers of migrants from other destinations, but also of dropping interest in transatlantic settlement among Europeans, especially from the European Union/EFTA/EEA countries.[3] An overview provided by the Migration Policy Institute has found that the total number of European Union-born immigrants in the US has decreased since the 1960s (Sumption and Hu 2011), while Weinar reached the same conclusion for the Canadian case (Weinar 2019). In general, Europeans apply less for permanent residency and their migration strategies no longer reflect intended. These characteristics do change from country to country, both of origin and destination. And thus, in the US case, there is no clear distinction between EU-15 or EU-12: in all groups there are countries with higher and lower numbers of permanent emigrants (Sumption and Hu 2011). This dynamic is quite different in the case of Canada, where the EU-15 are more likely to immigrate to Canada than the EU-13 (Weinar 2019).

However, lower numbers of permanent, settlement migration does not mean that overall mobility has fallen. In fact, a high share of Europeans still come to North America, but rather as temporary migrants. Sumption sums them up as scientists, managers, and tourists. These three categories reflect the main streams of entry: as workers in the knowledge economy (scientists and researchers); temporary workers in skilled positions; tourists. To this group, MPI added students, the number of which has increased over the last two decades. A closer look into the administrative data shows that EU citizens have been more prone to temporary migration since the 1980s. Their overall share has fallen, but they still keep their dominance in some categories of temporary work programs. For example, as noted by Sumption, "in 2005 EU-27 nationals received 15 percent of H-1B visas issued in US consulates abroad, 27 percent of L visas for intracompany transferees, and 53 percent of the

---

[1] https://medium.com/migration-issues/why-are-americans-leaving-75fe530ce49d [accessed 5 May 2019]. https://unstats.un.org/unsd/Demographic/meetings/egm/migrationegm06/DOC%20 19%20ILO.pdf#page=4 [accessed 5 May 2019].

[2] See e.g. https://www.nationalgeographic.com/culture/2018/07/graphic-united-states-immigration-origins-rings-tree-culture/ [accessed 5 May 2019].

[3] https://www.migrationpolicy.org/article/european-immigrants-united-states [accessed 5 May 2019].

most elite temporary work visas for individuals with "extraordinary ability" in the sciences, business, or arts (the O-1 visa). By 2009 Europeans' share of H-1B and L visa issuances had fallen slightly (to 10% and 23% respectively), but their share in O-1 visas has remained unchanged." (2011, p. 9).

A similar trajectory can be found in Canada. Most of the European Union citizens entering the country come as temporary migrants in just two programs: 52% in the International Mobility Program (for cultural and scientific exchanges and work and travel program IEC – International Experience Canada), and 19% are students. In fact, well over 42,700 EU nationals qualified for IEC in 2014 alone. Similar trends have been observed in the US (ESSQR 2014).

The stream for permanent residency was 20% of the total mobility, and came mostly from economic migration of skilled workers. Indeed, in 2016, the British, French, and Irish figured prominently among the top ten nationalities of Express Entry invitees, a program targeting highly skilled immigrants for permanent residency. Together they constituted 11% of all ITAs recipients. Under the Canadian point system, in that year the program privileged, through the assignment of maximum points, previous employment relationship applicants had Canadian employers or job offers in hand. In 2017, when the existing employment relationships in Canada and existing Canadian job offers were downgraded in the criteria (obtained fewer points), members of those same nationalities received only 5% of all invitations. The high share from 2016 is directly related to the quite high temporary migration of EU nationals to Canada, who come to the country on visitor visas or temporary work permits and thus have a chance to establish employment relations in Canada. This in turn, in 2016 at least, gave them heads-up in the Express Entry applications.

The most important take-away from the data analyzed both by Sumption and Weinar is that mechanisms of international mobility have replaced settlement migration in the transatlantic migration system. In the twenty-first century so far, temporary mobility has been double or triple the volume of the mobility for permanent residency, with over a million EU nationals engaging in various forms of temporary work or study in the US and Canada every year.

This data also attests to the fact that Europeans nowadays might have more social, financial, or human capital in order to make this immigration happen. But they also testify to the specificity of the transatlantic migration system in the twenty-first century, which has been transformed in a space of mobility.

4.3   Drivers of the Contemporary Mobility in the Transatlantic Context

In the view of growing globalization, since the mid-1990s scholars have been announcing the end of the nation-state, presumably weakened by globalisation. Sassen's "losing control" thesis concluded that the State can no longer fully control its borders (Sassen 1999). Two decades later the nation-state is back, with a vengeance. The nation-state is seen by some as the dominant actor in an international network that organises lives of individual people, citizens or not, by recreating the sense of belonging and translating it in freedom to move enshrined in identity documents and a variety of rights coming with them (Torpey 2000; Brubaker 1992). In the domestic context, the state is viewed as a guardian and guarantor of a rights framework (Bommes and Geddes 2000; Mau et al. 2012; Cholewinski and Taran 2009) while market powers are perceived as disruptors of this framework. From a point of view of immigration policy, the state is there to assure the rules of admission to the internal labour market and the rights framework for the workers. As the overarching institutional framework/actor entitled to use force, the state is also responsible for protecting own citizens against social dumping and unfair competition on the labour market (Coldron and Ackers 2009; Schmidt 2002). In many cases, it has an obligation to discriminate in favour of its own citizens. The key instruments the state has at its disposal to find the balance between these contradicting interests are the entry and residence regulations (hard barriers) and labour regulations understood as regulation of qualifications, skills and other requirements (soft barriers) (see also Chap. 3).

The intricate web of barriers and gateways is nowhere as evident as in the case of the modern transatlantic migration system. Over the last 50 years the states on both sides of the Atlantic have intensified collaboration in all spheres, built trade interdependence and gradually removed a number of barriers to mobility of the respective passport holders. Highly skilled migrants are one of the migrant groups and their rights are strictly related to the legal framework governing mobility within the transatlantic space, and most notably: to the power of their passports or what Spiro calls "premium citizenships" (Harpaz 2015). In what follows we discuss four groups of migrants, defined according to the number of hard and soft barriers to their mobility.

4.3.1 Open Border Migrants

This group is comprised of the citizens of the economic/political region of the European Union, who automatically gain mobility rights by holding the citizenship of another EU member state. Foreigners in this group can be called insiders, because their rights are on a par with the rights of citizens of the given member state. All hard barriers are removed for them, such as labour market access rights and welfare rights (long-term residence is contingent upon employment). Moreover, the soft barriers to their mobility are attenuated, based on multilateral or bilateral agreements which cover automatic recognition of educational credentials (thanks to the Bologna Process), clear rules of recognition of qualifications in regulated and non-regulated professions (thanks to EU-level legislation, e.g. Directive 2005/36/EC) and related mobility. Post-2008 economic crisis, migration from Southern to Northern Europe increased substantially (Lafleur and Stanek 2017), identifying both facilitation of recognition of qualifications as well as limitations (Klekowski von Koppenfels and Höhne 2017, pp. 167–8). Still, this internal group has not been open to all the countries in the transatlantic migration system and remains limited to the EU (Box 4.2).

> **Box 4.2: Intra-EU Mobility**
> Freedom of movement might be a double-edged sword in the transatlantic context. As research by Dominique Gross (2012) shows, when in 2002 Switzerland applied the EU freedom of movement, the policy had adverse effect on the size of high-skill immigration from North America. The priority given to Swiss and EU citizens pushed many highly skilled professionals to consider professional networks and financial opportunities back home. The consequent limitation of geographical heterogeneity in immigrants can be detrimental to Swiss businesses.

EU labour mobility delivers benefits for both sending and receiving countries. In a long-term perspective with increasing return flows, the distinction between sending and receiving can become blurred. With return flows being facilitated, diminishing regulations and enforcing mutual recognition, the original sending countries may benefits from present remittances whilst expecting future knowledge and innovation to come through returnees. Receiving countries enjoy a pool of talents to count on in booming times. This ensures that the business cycle avoids bottlenecks.

Rights of this insider group can be extended to non-EU passport holders under certain conditions inscribed in the immigration legislation of the EU and more specifically as regards Long Term Residents (LTRs), refugees and Blue Card recipients. This means that US citizens and Canadian citizens can only achieve full mobility on par with EU citizens when they become LTRs or Blue Card holders (refugee status is irrelevant in this case). However, a legal framework allowing for open borders, as in the EU, does not exist in North America.

4.3.2   Semi-open Borders Migrants

Aside from visa-waiver/visa-free entry between North America and (most) EU states, there is no legal framework that benefits European passport holders when emigrating to North America and vice versa. However, a number of arrangements do facilitate mobility and thus give a certain advantage to the transatlantic passport holders. States on both sides of the Atlantic have developed a number of channels to facilitate such entry for respective citizens, although the framework is not all-encompassing and we can see a patchwork of bilateral and multilateral arrangements.

What we might call the semi-open borders migrant group is comprised of citizens of the EU, US and Canada. Most of them (enjoy visa-free access to each other territory as visitors (business, tourists or job-seekers) for minimum 90 days (Weinar

2019; Sumption and Hu 2011). Moreover, some other hard barriers to mobility removed: e.g. the States assure their preferential treatment on the basis of the new generation of trade agreements (e.g. CETA) or special political relationship (e.g. Quebec and France); the States have built a network of agreements facilitating mobility of students and researchers (e.g. Fulbright-Schuman fellowships or the DAAD fellowship scheme). Citizens of the countries with special relationship gain automatic access rights to the labour market on stipulated terms, without quotas. It is notable that the transatlantic migration system is the one with the most work and travel agreements in the world (Weinar 2017).

The role of trade relations for this migrant category cannot be overstated. Increased economic relationships, with businesses active on both sides of the Atlantic, predominantly drive mobility of these skilled migrants. Most recently, the EU-Canada Comprehensive Economic Trade Agreement (CETA) devoted a whole chapter to the mobility of temporary workers. Chapter 10 of CETA provides for enhanced mobility for contractual services suppliers, independent professionals, and business people visiting for investment purposes, investors, and intra-corporate transferees (which includes senior personnel, specialists and graduate trainees). It does not preclude the use of the visas (Art. 10.3(3)), but it insists on a facilitated and reasonably quick way to get the documents needed in order to move. In effect, it states, the immigration procedures for the citizens of the parties to the agreement shall be prioritised, not to endanger the trade relations. Annex 10-E outlines over 50 sectors in which the mobility of service suppliers and independent professionals is to be facilitated. It also includes a long list of exclusions, almost entirely from the EU Member States, concerning labour market access, primarily related to the requirement of a labour market test, a rather standard, yet time-consuming procedure. The agreement looks quite unbalanced from this perspective, given that Canada includes nearly no exclusions.

In the semi-open borders scenario, the illusion of open borders is quickly dispelled when the migrants encounter the "soft barriers" to the labour market access and access to rights. These barriers usually keep the migrant workers in pre-defined sectors and occupations. However, in the transatlantic case, there have been clear attempts to remove these barriers. Chapter 11 of CETA invites parties to work towards the mutual recognition of qualifications. The language from this chapter has been modelled after the France-Québec Agreement on the Mutual Recognition of Qualifications (MRA). It sets out a general framework, detailed in Annex 11-A, on how to approach this. Recognition of qualifications has been facilitated also in other instances: Quebec-France MRA, or mutual understanding achieved by the professional bodies through decades of cooperation. In the first case, over 160 regulated professions and trades have had clear translation schemes established for them (Weinar et al. 2017). Thanks to the agreement, skilled French workers (permanent and temporary) experience shorter delays in pursuing their profession in Quebec. The agreement minimises the likelihood of deskilling for French citizens, and thus prevents the brain-waste in the event they return to France. In the second case, the qualifications of many UK-trained professionals are recognized more easily in

Canada or the US thanks to the organic work of professional bodies of the two juris-dictions that span decades of bilateral relations (Iredale 2001; Weinar 2019).

Finally, migrants in this group benefit from a dense net of treaties which avoid dual taxation and which support combined approach to social security (Sumption and Hu 2011). Overall, we can say that the arrangements in place, albeit not encom-passing all countries in the transatlantic migration system equally, create a sphere of increased mobility, especially in the short-term.

4.3.3   Selected Temporary Migrants

Transatlantic migration system also has a number of exclusions. The selected migrants group is made up of citizens of the other countries, outside of the EU/US/CAN system. The decision to allow for more mobility rights is usually limited in scope and can take a form of a unilateral policy or bilateral arrangement (proposed however by the receiving country). The programs allow for entry of temporary workers under very specific conditions, often within set quotas. Their entry to the labour market is narrowly defined and thus "hard" and "soft barriers" create a sec-ondary class of migrants. All temporary worker programs for low-skilled migrants fall in this category, e.g. in the EU we are talking about seasonal migration, in the US and Canada: temporary workers in agriculture. Yet, highly skilled workers are also a part of the temporary foreign workers stream, e.g. as H1B visa holders in the US or International Mobility Program beneficiaries in Canada. Their presence is however less visible and not mediatised.

There are also a number of educational exchanges between Europe and the United States, including Fulbright, DAAD (German Academic Exchange Service) and many others. These are, however, often conceptualized as programs for cultural understanding rather than explicit training or temporary high-skilled worker pro-grams. Nonetheless, as having lived abroad is a predictor for aspiring to live abroad again (Marrow and Klekowski von Koppenfels 2020: 28), such programmes do contribute to future mobility.

4.3.4   Closed Borders

The closed borders of the transatlantic system is the reality faced by the majority of the world population. Mobility under these circumstances is impossible. Permanent migration pathways are open to a small share of potentially interested individuals in North America, and inexistent in Europe, as all legal immigrants to European Union are initially temporary migrants, but can transition to a permanent status. Those who cannot make it through the bottlenecked legal channels try other ways in. As a result, undocumented flows of migrants then become vulnerable migrant workers, exploited or even enslaved (Bales 2012; Callister et al. 2006). Only few EU/US/

CAN citizens emerge in this group (Weinar 2019; Sumption and Hu 2011) perhaps particularly so in the case of bilateral flows between European Union and North America, although some migrants from the Global North may well be undocumented.

Drivers of mobility in the transatlantic migration system are thus related to economic and political cooperation that has developed in this area over the last 100 years. The transatlantic migration system is organised by state power networks that regulate mobilities of citizens within them (Krahmann 2005; Paár-Jákli 2014). The ascent of the European Union with its bold ideas of open borders for goods, services and people has influenced the bilateral policies. The idea of beneficial influence of people-to-people contacts and profits brought by mobility of certain workers to the transnational businesses has shaped the transatlantic space as we know it today. The openness allowed more people to move and not emigrate for life, especially in the face of the similar growth and wealth of the countries involved. Mass migration was removed from the equation after World War II and even the recent financial crisis has not led to a dramatic increase in settlement migration nor mobility (Weinar 2019; Sumption and Hu 2011). Still, skilled migrants from both sides of the Atlantic are usually more apt in finding ways to increase their mobility while minimising risks. They benefit disproportionately from arrangements based on economic relations, to be sure, but they also know well how to use them to their advantage. Having no organisation which would support them, they analyse their options offered by the opportunity structure created within the transatlantic space and use their networks to move their social/financial/cultural capital with a lower risk during bi-directional or circular movements over the Atlantic (Weinar 2019; Klekowski von Koppenfels 2014; Bauder et al. 2017). The insights to the privileged position of these migrants in this system can be further gathered when applying intersectional analysis (Kaushik and Walsh 2018). Such analysis, derived from feminist studies, looks at experience of the same category of immigrants through the lens of gender, class, and race/ethnicity. Studies elsewhere have shown the special position of OECD migrants, especially if white, for whom the settlement (and related belonging) is facilitated by privileges of race, class and visa policy (Callister et al. 2006; Boucher 2007). A density and vibrancy of the transatlantic migration system can only amplify this dynamic.

How can we thus make sense of the transatlantic highly skilled migrants? Indeed, they form a quite specific group, clearly different from all other groups of migrants, including highly skilled migrants in other migration systems.

4.4 Highly Skilled as Agents in Their Own Lives – A Northerners' Story

The unique opportunity structures in the transatlantic context explain the prevalence of short-term mobility. However, we know little as to what prompts some of the highly skilled migrants to settle or return.

Indeed, as noted by Altbach, according to the National Academy of Science's Survey of Earned Doctorates (SED) in the US, the countries with the most impressive economic and educational expansion seem to be those with the most share of settlers' rates, around the year 2011. The study cites the various dynamics characterising the propensity to stay per region of origin. According to it, three decades ago over a quarter of Chinese doctoral graduates were returning to China immediately after completing their degrees, while in early 2000s this rate dropped to just over 7%. Similar downward trend has been noted for the Indian graduates in the US (13–10%). Yet, return rates vary considerably, ranging from 84% of Thais, 60% of Mexicans and Brazilians, and 39.5% of Africans (Altbach 2013).

As regards European return rates from the US, they have been measured by van Bouwel in a pioneering quantitative study analysing the behaviour of a sample of PhD students in economics (Van Bouwel 2010). Van Bouwel found a high stay rate of 64% for those who find employment upon the completion of their degrees, while 18% returns immediately to their home countries. However, some portion of stayers chose to return later, usually before receiving a tenured position or if they are unable to secure one, increasing thus the overall return rate to 24%. Interestingly enough, close to 11% move to another European country, most often to the UK. This choice is often the preferred one for Italians and Germans in particular.

Another set of data provided by the author focused on the regional disparities between the returnees. Not surprisingly, return rates are lower for the researchers from Eastern Europe: 6% for the first job, and 14% for the second job. The scientific and research environment in these countries can explain the reluctance of the young researchers to come back. Also, the differences in real salaries (purchasing power) do not favour return. Also it seems that the experience in the US does not bring enough return-to-investment benefit on the Eastern European labour markets. In consequence, as the author notes, it seems that these researchers perceive their student migration to the US as a more permanent move, whereas researchers from richer western European countries have a higher tendency of regarding it as temporary. On the other side of the spectrum are the researchers from Scandinavian countries and Southern European countries, where the return rates are higher than average, at 24% and 23% for the return for the first job, respectively. They are even higher for the second job, 32% and 30%, respectively. In the case of Greece, these numbers reached 56% for the second job. These high shares can be explained by the good working conditions in Scandinavian countries, leading the technological breakthroughs in Europe, as well as their social security systems. In the case of Southern Europe, the author explains the high return rates by the cultural and family ties, as well as the high return to investment on the North American experience on the job market (Van Bouwel 2010).

This rather simple quantitative exercise shows already the complexity of factors that can push a migrant to return home, to move onward, or to settle. More qualitative work has helped us delve deeper into the meanders of the migrating decisions.

First element to consider is the propensity to move. What do we know about the mobility of highly skilled migrants across the Atlantic in twenty-first century? The data, cited above, prove that the circularity or temporariness is what defines the migratory dynamics. But qualitative studies show that this mobility is not limited to the transatlantic space for some of the highly skilled migrants. There are in fact several categories of migrants, for whom mobility is way of life and the move over the Pond is one of many they perform. Weinar (2019) presents the results of the qualitative survey of the EU citizens living outside of the EU and observes that for the majority a non-EU destination was their second or third migratory experience. In her sample, many participants were secondary migrants or even serial migrants: nearly 40% had resided for longer than 6 months in one country other than Canada. Forty-six percent of those repeated migrants had engaged exclusively in intra-EU mobility prior to emigrating outside of the European Union, with 33% of this group living in one other EU country, while 12% had lived in more than two. Many participants had also experienced serial mobility outside of the EU. Twenty-seven percent migrated both to EU and non-EU countries, while the same share (27%) migrated only to non-EU countries. A history of extreme multiple migrations was indicated by 8% of respondents, who had lived in five different countries other than their country of citizenship. Among non-EU destinations, the transatlantic space was dominating, with US and Canada accounting for over 50% of all non-EU countries of previous residence (Box 4.3).

> **Box 4.3: Middle Class and Middling Migrants**
> Ball and Nikita define the global middle class as "managers and professionals and their families who move around the globe in the employ of multi-national corporations (MNCs) or as free-lance experts" (Ball and Nikita 2014, p. 85). "Middling migrants" (Conradson and Latham 2005) can be people who migrate on their own as students, skilled workers or spouses and offer their skills on a foreign labour market. In these cases, even if they may not face the discrimination with which lower-skilled workers might be confronted, they do not have the protection of a multinational company's human resource department and may enjoy little actual privilege in the host countries' legal systems. Like many other migrants, they also face the additional constraints of immigration systems or precarious work arrangements (Luthra and Platt 2016). The precariousness is often at the heart of serial mobility, where a migrant's drive to maximise their skills, balanced against fear of losing them, becomes a perpetual trap of changing places and countries.

It is important to say that in the case of the extreme multiple migrants, none were employees of multinational companies and less than 2% were employed by international organisations. Majority had organised the moves by themselves, usually starting with an international student experience and then moving through a series of international employment opportunities. These highly skilled migrants have been called in the literature professional lifestyle travellers (or self-initiated expatriates/self-initiated global careerists in management literature) as they use their profession or skills to move between the countries (Ho 2011; Mäkelä and Suutari 2013;

Eich-Krohm 2012). They are not tied down by a permanent employment contract or a particular company, they are relatively free to move around. More often than not they can be assigned to the "middling migrant" category, as people belonging to the transatlantic middle class and simply using the opportunity structures that lower the risks of international mobility.

That agency of the migrant is the key to understand the mobility sequences. Although all migrants have this agency and control the decision about their move, the transatlantic migration system is the only system in which the risks of the mobility have been substantially lowered and migrants can see their plans through, with only some outcomes left to the factors out of their control. This situation creates a different scale against which we can measure the success of migration. When the risk is lower, the expectations of succeeding are just higher. Most importantly, the success is rarely defined by the sheer ability to settle and stay (Weinar 2019). The expectations are higher as regards the access to the labour market, for example, or the lifestyle. Ability to move and enjoy the benefits mobility can bring, in terms of new skills and experiences, is often seen as a measure of success. At the same time, concepts of "home" or "return" are ambivalent.

Only a few scholars have looked recently at the transatlantic migration and have tried to understand qualitatively the dynamics of mobility and settlement. The scarce literature at our disposal sheds the light on the settlement decision of the twenty-first century transatlantic migrant, in both directions.

Weinar (2019) looked specifically at European immigrants coming to North America in recent decades, with a specific interest in the tension between mobility and settlement among the highly skilled while Klekowski von Koppenfels (2014) studied US citizens living in Europe. On both accounts, the authors found several regularities in the migrants' behaviour and migration patterns. Among the US citizens studied by Klekowski von Koppenfels, nearly all of whom were highly skilled in the sense of having tertiary education, joining a partner was the primary proximate reason for migration. In terms of migration aspiration, however, a more recent study shows that working abroad and study abroad both rank ahead of joining a partner (Marrow and Klekowski von Koppenfels 2020, p. 11), suggesting that there is variation between an intended reason for migration and the proximate migration motivator. Marrow and Klekowski von Koppenfels also found that, as education levels declined, US citizens were more likely to indicate migration aspiration in order to join a partner (2018, p. 26), although higher levels of education did not predict higher levels of aspiration to migrate. Having previously lived abroad had a positive affect on individuals' propensity to aspire to migrate, while having social networks with Americans who had lived abroad was significant for predicting migration aspiration (Marrow and Klekowski von Koppenfels 2020, p. 28).

Similarly, for twenty-first century European migrants in Canada, they had usually lived in some other country before deciding on a longer transatlantic move. Most of them actually had been to the country for a shorter visit before migration, they knew the language and had at least some idea about the environment. However, these same people had less propensity to decide for final settlement in Canada. In the Canadian case especially, the interviewed Europeans came as short-term migrants (students or temporary workers) and then changed their status to permanent residency; Klekowski von Koppenfels observed this same tendency among US citizens in Europe, dubbing them "accidental migrants" (2014, p. 43). However, for the Europeans in Canada, the achievement of permanent residence status did not preclude the idea of further mobility or return to Europe, if not necessarily the home country. Still, not only the return to home country was not a priority for over 50% of the interviewees; they were rather thinking about moving to another EU country or another country outside of the EU. These immigrants had proven beyond doubt that they do not shy away from mobility, understand its mechanics, and can follow on their initial plans. Their mobility is not contingent upon limiting economic factors; they do not face drastic differences of economic opportunities upon return. The decision to stay or move is rather related with their life-course. Indeed, the life-course analysis seems to be crucial in the case of highly skilled transatlantic migrants; Klekowski von Koppenfels also observed for US citizens in Europe that a return to the US was most likely in the case of a need to care for ageing parents, whilst an onward move was rather linked to exciting and advantageous employment opportunities (2014).

In Weinar's study, the temporary movers are usually in their twenties or thirties. The decision to settle for longer (and this might include getting a citizenship) or to move on/return happens in their 40s. This can be explained by the family-related factors and career-development factors.

Life course events have been recognized as playing a role in affecting both migration decisions and migration trajectories; highly skilled migrants are no different (see, e.g. Ho 2011; Bailey and Mulder 2017). The life-course of a citizen of an industrialised country has changed over the last 100 years. In the twenty-first century, families tend to be more atomic and to expand later in the lifetime of a person, so in their thirties migrants - like others in industrialized countries - only start thinking about having children and settling down. And even having young children is not necessarily a factor enhancing the likelihood of settlement. Moving countries with small children has become much easier in the transatlantic space, with very similar educational and social security systems, so the decision on where the "home" is can be delayed, usually until the schooling age of the children. Indeed, interviewed migrants who were in couples had quite flexible view of the notion of "home". In 80% of cases, they were escaping the strictly diasporic life, often coming back into the fold only for the language schooling of their children. If the migrants came to the new country as a family with children, they focused on the positive impact the move would have on them: new language and cultural skills. These families were curious of other cultures and embraced the idea of living in a global world that offers so much more than just one country. Especially in the US study, many of the presented families were clearly mobile families, who enjoyed the "on the move" lifestyle.

In the transatlantic space, settlement in North America in the case of North American-European couples is not a given. Klekowski von Koppenfels found that over half of her survey respondents in a committed relationship had a partner with European citizenship (2014, p. 101); decisions about where to live depended on a number of factors, including family ties and employment opportunities. While "love migration" (e.g. Mai and King 2009) is certainly an important factor in transatlantic migration, it does not preclude employment - of Klekowski von Koppenfels' US citizen survey respondents in Europe, just under 7% were not employed and not looking for work (2014, p. 80). It is important to note that with partners who both hold "valued" citizenships, and who are both highly-skilled, a wider variety of options in terms of migration and settlement are open. As for professional development, migrating to North America often involves getting new skills or academic credentials to expand the existing career. If the professional situation crystallises by the third year in the North American context, the initial temporary migrants get more clarity about their settlement preferences. Most of the applications for the status change are submitted in the second or third year of the temporary stay (Weinar 2019). Indeed, in the Canadian case, many companies hiring temporary workers from Europe advise them to apply for the permanent residence permit. Interestingly enough, not all do that, even in the face of the offered sponsorship, as many have in their heads progressive career goals that include global mobility beyond Canada (Weinar 2019).

Some scholars describe the decision to settle in a country of destination as the result of interactive multi-level factors, which involve family and career, but also other variables, such as standard of living (Benson and O'Reilly 2009), perceived dynamics of the city they live in (Leslie and Brail 2011), or the level of welfare (Habti 2019). In the case of scientists, some raised the importance of the scientific and technological infrastructure being equally important as the quality of life (Siekierski et al. 2018). Canadian researchers have been especially invested in this type of research, as for two decades now they have been reporting systematic dissatisfaction among the highly skilled migrants with their immigration to Canada (Sapeha 2015). Interestingly enough, the satisfaction with settlement has been associated with integration into the ethnically diverse group, while ethnic enclaves are associated with dissatisfaction. In particular many researchers demonstrated that racial minorities tend to integrate into the Canadian society slower than minorities of European background, what can be associated with the fact that they face less discrimination and thus are more easily welcome into the multi ethnic circles (Sapeha 2015; Reitz 2005; Reitz et al. 2009). In all contexts, highly skilled immigrants from Europe are the ones who are more prone to express their intention to move rather than stay, or have more doubts. Employment satisfaction and the life style are two the most important elements driving the decision to stay.

While there has been a tendency in some literature to identify all migrants from the Global North as lifestyle migrants, we would point out that this group is somewhat less present in the transatlantic space. For North Americans moving to Central America or Mexico, or Northern Europeans moving to southern Spain or France, the classic lifestyle migrant profile can certainly apply -- those who leave their countries in search of a better quality of life, often defined in terms of cheaper living costs, milder weather, or a more relaxed lifestyle (Benson and O'Reilly 2009; Benson and Osbaldiston 2014; Cohen et al. 2015; Korpela 2014). While interwar Paris represented a certain lifestyle, with the US dollar then going much further in

Paris than it does in 2019, today, lifestyle migration involves other dimensions, many of which are not limited to migrants from the Global North or, indeed, to highly skilled migrants: But the lifestyle choices can involve other dimensions nowadays: access to exciting professional careers or a more technically challenging employment, providing children with additional cultural capital, exposure to new cultures. Lifestyle migration is better thought of as a part of a continuum, rather than as a distinct category; clearly much lifestyle migration is undertaken by highly-skilled migrants, but we caution that by no means are all highly-skilled migrants to be dubbed lifestyle migrants. Indeed, Benson and Osbaldiston caution that "as a label [lifestyle migration] is adopted uncritically and rarely problematized by authors" (Benson and Osbaldiston 2016, p. 409). We note that such lifestyle migration can apply to technically skilled migrants as well as those who are professionals, or highly skilled migrants migrating after their productive years, that is, for retirement. Yet, like many other terms in use in migration research, the term lifestyle migration.

4.5   Brain Flows in the Transatlantic Context

As discussed in Chap. 3, the impacts of highly skilled migration on countries of origin and destination can have various facets. In the transatlantic context, issues of brain drain have not been studied in any systematic way in the last 50 years or so. There is a widely shared acceptance of the fact that the "brain trade" (Franzoni et al. 2012) between the two regions has been balanced.

The only area where some studies have emerged is the area of knowledge transfers between origin and destination, as researched by economists (Breschi et al. 2017; Bhagwati and Hanson 2009).

In general, the knowledge transfers, or "brain gain effects," "brain circulation" or "brain flows" have been divided into three, non-mutually exclusive categories:

1. Ethnic-driven' knowledge flows, where the highly skilled migrants use their social networks to promote new ideas among their peers in the country of origin (Meyer 2001).
2. Knowledge transfers facilitated by the mobility within the multinational companies (Blomström and Kokko 1998; Veugelers and Cassiman 2004).
3. Direct impact of the returnees, who use their new skills in their professional life (e.g. students or young professionals) or who engage in new entrepreneurial activities or research activities (e.g. start-ups, research projects) relying on their professional networks at destination (Argote and Ingram 2000).

More specifically, transatlantic economic and social space has been a scene of unique and intense dynamic of two-ways flows of finance, goods, and people. The mutual exchanges of capital and ideas are unquestionable and even taken for granted. It seems to be common sense that all of these three phenomena take place between North America and Europe, but surprisingly, not much research is done to investigate more in depth the ramifications of such strong bonds, even if such a deep understanding could prepare the field for more insightful research into other, emerging, spaces of mobility. The economists working on the questions of brain flows focus predominantly on South-North migrations, and less so on intra-OECD movements.

However, the specificities of the transatlantic mobility makes it very difficult for economists to measure the impacts on the countries of origin and destination. In particular, the lack of consistent datasets on temporary mobility is the major obstacle. As noted by Breschi and colleagues, economists have it easier to study the various impacts of the mobility of Chinese and Indian highly skilled to the US because of the robust data linked to the immigration/emigration status and important real numbers of H1B and J-1 visa recipients from these countries (Breschi et al. 2017). And this is even in the light of the official OECD immigration data, which shows that some European countries are systematically among the top 10 contributors to the stock of highly educated migrants within the OECD, and most notably the UK, Germany and Poland. Indeed, as Breschi et al. noted, the combined stock of these three countries was 60% higher than that of India (top of the ranking) and more than twice that of China in 2011. In their study, the team has thus taken to include several European countries in their rather isolated attempt to build and analyse an extensive dataset of US-based foreign-origin inventors and their knowledge transfers. The category of scientists is not well represented in the official immigration data, i.e. the J-1 category visa data can be misleading, as it covers visitors in various fields and various roles in the broad science and cultural cooperation field, not necessarily inventors. H-1B visa data is even less representative, as it is primarily focusing on temporary highly skilled workers, who however sometimes can be employed in research institutions and develop inventions. In creating their novel dataset, Breschi and colleagues used the EP-INV, a database of uniquely identified inventors listed on patent applications at the European Patent Office (EPO), and combined it with the name analysis based on IBM-GNR, a commercial database. In their analysis, foreign origin inventors include both foreign nationals and US citizens of ethnic origins (both naturalised and US-born). They used an interesting proxy for knowledge transfer, namely forward citations by other scientists related to the patent applications deposed by these inventors. They define the "diaspora effect" as the phenomenon whereby a US-resident inventors of the same ethnic origin have a higher propensity to cite one another's patents, compared with patents by other inventors, other things being equal. They also attempted to see the "brain gain effect", and they defined it as a phenomenon whereby US-resident inventors are disproportionately cited by inventors in their countries of origin. They found diaspora effect almost inexistent in the case of most of the studied European nationalities (Polish, French, and Italian), with some minor effect for German scientists. As regards brain gain effect, the team found that it is quite low, almost inexistent. They concluded that more direct transfers of knowledge, such as co-invention networks and professional networks run by multinational companies have more direct effect. Still, any systematic research in this field has not been developed.

The vast field of research focusing on knowledge transfers in the transatlantic context seem to be created in a total disjunction with the field of migration studies, and does not look at all into the questions of human capital transferability, brain gain or diaspora effects related to migration (Versailles and Mérindol 2006; Allen et al. 2007; Carayannis and Campbell 2006; DeBardeleben and Leblond 2011). Specifically, some authors have attempted analysis of co-inventions in the EU-US context (Carayannis and Laget 2004) but they have not engaged in the analysis of possible role of diaspora networks or short-term mobility, disregarding the actual policy and social environment in which these collaborations could develop and happen. As an unintended consequence, they rather provide a rich picture of short-term motilities of highly skilled migrants across the Atlantic, without really linking previous mobility experience to the intensity of international collaborations.

Another element worth looking at, when talking about impacts on the economic development on both sides of the Atlantic, is the impact on trade. In this case, the overarching studies are rather inexistent. The somewhat general acknowledgement of the impact immigration has on Canada has been offered by the Government of Canada on the contribution of multiculturalism to trade (Government of Canada 2002). Yet, even the studies supporting the negotiations of CETA disregarded the impact of the diasporic or ethnic businesses in the growth of EU-Canada trade. The same can be said about the US case. The research field is atomised and focuses on specific ethnic groups rather than taking an overarching approach to European-North American economic relations through the lens of longer and shorter term mobility of the highly skilled migrants (Anderson 2006).

4.6 Conclusions

Transatlantic migration flows have been the cradle of migration studies. The transatlantic migration system is by far the most developed and the busiest in the twenty-first century. As such it can serve as a laboratory for researchers to test hypotheses and look for trends that will define human mobility tomorrow. At the same time, this migration system has changed substantially over the decades, and diversification of migration flows is the rule, rather than the exception. The mobility of the highly skilled is a case in point – they are the dominant migrant group in the transatlantic space nowadays. They cross the Atlantic in both directions, in different ways: as economic immigrants, as temporary visitors, as service providers, as students and as spouses/partners. They use available opportunity structures and enjoy lower risk mobility for professional or individual development. If they decide to settle, it is often because of their consideration of the specific context: lifestyle, professional opportunities. The classic ideas of wage differentials are no longer a decisive factor shaping the decision to stay. Moreover, even if settled for several years or more, the transatlantic migrants are prone to secondary migrations, return or forward. This extreme mobility reflects the future of all global migrations.

Since the research on transatlantic migrations has not yet been fully developed, we know very little about the actual economic impact the highly skilled might have on the economies at origin and destination. We know a lot about the state of collaboration and knowledge transfers between North America and Europe, but we cannot say with any certainty whether there is a brain drain or brain gain effect in this context. This is in contrast to studies on South-North migrations, where the impact of highly skilled migration is assessed in depth, especially on the countries of origin (see Chap. 3). This persistent gap in research is one of several that should be addressed in further research.

References

Allen, J., James, A. D., & Gamlen, P. (2007). Formal versus informal knowledge networks in R&D: A case study using social network analysis. *R&D Management, 37*(3), 179–196.

Altbach, P. G. (2013). The complexities of 21st-century brain exchange. In P. G. Altbach (Ed.), *The international imperative in higher education* (Global perspectives on higher education) (pp. 47–50). Rotterdam: Sense Publishers. https://doi.org/10.1007/978-94-6209-338-6_11.

Anderson, G. (2006). *Networks of contact: The Portuguese and Toronto.* Waterloo: Wilfrid Laurier University Press.

Argote, L., & Ingram, P. (2000). Knowledge transfer: A basis for competitive advantage in firms. *Organizational Behavior and Human Decision Processes, 82*(1), 150–169.

Bailey, A., & Mulder, C. H. (2017). Highly skilled migration between the global north and south: Gender, life courses and institutions. *Journal of Ethnic and Migration Studies, 43*(16), 2689–2703. https://doi.org/10.1080/1369183X.2017.1314594.

Bales, K. (2012). *Disposable people: New slavery in the global economy* (Updated with a new preface). Berkeley: University of California Press.

Ball, S. J., & Nikita, D. P. (2014). The global middle class and school choice: A cosmopolitan sociology. *Zeitschrift für Erziehungswissenschaft, 17*(3), 81–93.

Bauder, H., Hannan, C.-A., & Lujan, O. (2017). International experience in the academic field: Knowledge production, symbolic capital, and mobility fetishism. *Population, Space and Place, 23*(6), e2040. https://doi.org/10.1002/psp.2040.

Benson, M., & O'Reilly, K. (2009). Migration and the search for a better way of life: A critical exploration of lifestyle migration. *The Sociological Review, 57*(4), 608–625.

Benson, M., & Osbaldiston, N. (2014). New horizons in lifestyle migration research: Theorising movement, settlement and the search for a better way of life. In *Understanding Lifestyle Migration* (pp. 1–23). London: Springer.

Benson, M., & Osbaldiston, N. (2016). Toward a critical sociology of lifestyle migration: Reconceptualizing migration and the search for a better way of life. *The Sociological Review, 64*(3), 407–423.

Bhagwati, J. N., & Hanson, G. H. (2009). *Skilled immigration today: Prospects, problems, and policies* (Vol. 17). Oxford: Oxford University Press Oxford.

Blomström, M., & Kokko, A. (1998). Multinational corporations and Spillovers. *Journal of Economic Surveys, 12*(3), 247–277.

Bommes, M., & Geddes, A. (2000). *Immigration and welfare: Challenging the Borders of the welfare state* (Vol. 1). London: Psychology Press.

Boucher, A. (2007). Skill, migration and gender in Australia and Canada: The case of gender-based analysis. *Australian Journal of Political Science, 42*(3), 383–401.

Breschi, S., Lissoni, F., & Miguelez, E. (2017). Foreign-origin inventors in the USA: Testing for diaspora and brain gain effects. *Journal of Economic Geography, 17*(5), 1009–1038. https://doi.org/10.1093/jeg/lbw044.

Brimm, L. (2010). *Global cosmopolitans: The creative edge of difference.* Basingstoke: Springer.

Brubaker, R. (1992). *Nationhood and citizenship in France and Germany.* Cambridge, MA: Harvard University Press.

Callister, P., Bedford, R., Didham, R. A., & Statistics New Zealand. (2006). *Globalisation, gendered migration and labour markets.* Department of Labour.

Carayannis, E. G., & Campbell, D. F. J. (2006). *Knowledge creation, diffusion, and use in innovation networks and knowledge clusters: A comparative systems approach across the United States, Europe, and Asia.* Santa Barbara: Greenwood Publishing Group.

Carayannis, E. G., & Laget, P. (2004). Transatlantic innovation infrastructure networks: Public-private, EU–US R&D Partnerships. *R&D Management, 34*(1), 17–31.

Cholewinski, R., & Taran, P. (2009). Migration, governance and human rights: Contemporary dilemmas in the era of globalization. *Refugee Survey Quarterly, 28*(4), 1–33. https://doi.org/10.1093/rsq/hdq019.

Cohen, S. A., Duncan, T., & Thulemark, M. (2015). Lifestyle Mobilities: The crossroads of travel, leisure and migration. *Mobilities, 10*(1), 155–172. https://doi.org/10.1080/17450101.2013.826481.

Coldron, K., & Ackers, L. (2009). European citizenship, individual agency and the challenge to social welfare systems: A case study of retirement migration in the European Union. *Policy & Politics, 37*(4), 573–589.

Conradson, D., & Latham, A. (2005). Transnational urbanism: Attending to everyday practices and Mobilities. *Journal of Ethnic and Migration Studies, 31*(2), 227–233. https://doi.org/10.1080/1369183042000339891.

DeBardeleben, J., & Leblond, P. (2011). The other transatlantic relationship: Canada, the EU, and 21st-century challenges. *International Journal, 66*(1), 1–7.

Franzoni, C., Scellato, G., & Stephan, P. (2012). Foreign-born scientists: Mobility patterns for 16 countries. *Nature Biotechnology, 30*(12), 1250.

Habti, D. (2019). What's driving migrant Russian physicians to stay permanently in Finland? A life-course approach. *Journal of Finnish Studies, 22*(1/2), 85–118.

Eich-Krohm, A. (2012). *German professionals in the United States: A gendered analysis of the migration decision of highly skilled families.* El Paso: LFB Scholarly Publishing.

ESSQR. (2014). *EU Employment and Social Situation*, Quarterly Review, June 2014, Supplement on Mobility. DG EMPL, European Commission.

Gabaccia, D. R. (2013). *Italy's many diasporas.* Routledge.

Gross, D. M. (2012). Free mobility with the EU and immigration of North American brains to Switzerland. *Swiss Journal of Economics and Statistics, 148*(4), 497–530.

Government of Canada, Public Services and Procurement Canada. (2002, July 1). Multiculturalism: Its contribution to Canada's international trade and investment activities/Hon. Mark Eyking, Chair.: XC75-1/1-421-10E-PDF – Government of Canada Publications – Canada.Ca." http://publications.gc.ca/site/eng/9.856130/publication.html

Harpaz, Y. (2015). Ancestry into opportunity: How global inequality drives demand for long-distance European Union citizenship. *Journal of Ethnic and Migration Studies, 41*(13), 2081–2104.

Ho, E. L.-E. (2011). Migration trajectories of 'highly skilled' middling Transnationals: Singaporean Transmigrants in London. *Population, Space and Place, 17*(1), 116–129. https://doi.org/10.1002/psp.569.

Iredale, R. (2001). The internationalization of professionals and the assessment of skills: Australia, Canada and the US. *Georgetown Immigration Law Journal, 16*, 797.

Kaushik, V., & Walsh, C. A. (2018). A critical analysis of the use of Intersectionality theory to understand the settlement and integration needs of skilled immigrants to Canada. *Canadian Ethnic Studies, 50*(3), 27–47. https://doi.org/10.1353/ces.2018.0021.

Klekowski von Koppenfels, A. (2014). *Migrants or expatriates?: Americans in Europe.* New York: Springer.

Koppenfels, A. K. v., & Höhne, J. (2017). Gastarbeiter migration revisited: Consolidating Germany's position as an immigration country. In *South-north migration of EU citizens in times of crisis* (pp. 149–174). Cham: Springer.

Korpela, M. (2014). Lifestyle of freedom? Individualism and lifestyle migration. In *Understanding lifestyle migration* (pp. 27–46). London: Springer.

Krahmann, E. (2005). Security governance and networks: New theoretical perspectives in transatlantic security. *Cambridge Review of International Affairs, 18*(1), 15–30.

Lafleur, Jean-Michel, and Mikolaj Stanek. (2017). South-north migration of EU citizens in times of crisis.

Leslie, D., & Brail, S. (2011). The productive role of 'quality of place': A case study of fashion designers in Toronto. *Environment and Planning A: Economy and Space, 43*(12), 2900–2917. https://doi.org/10.1068/a43473.

Luthra, R., & Platt, L. (2016). Elite or middling? International students and migrant diversification. *Ethnicities, 16*(2), 316–344. https://doi.org/10.1177/1468796815616155.

Mai, N., & King, R. (2009). Love, sexuality and migration: Mapping the issue (s). *Mobilities, 4*(3), 295–307.

Mäkelä, K., & Suutari, V. (2013). The work-life Interface of self-initiated expatriates: Conflicts and enrichment. In *Talent Management of Self-Initiated Expatriates: A Neglected Source of Global Talent.* Basingstoke: Palgrave Macmillan.

Marrow, H. B., & Koppenfels, A. K. v. (2020). Modeling American migration aspirations: How capital, race, and National Identity Shape Americans' ideas about living abroad. *International Migration Review, 54*(1), 83–119.

Mau, S., Brabandt, H., Laube, L., & Roos, C. (2012). *Liberal states and the freedom of movement: Selective Borders, unequal mobility.* Basingstoke: Palgrave Macmillan.

Meier, L. (2014). *Migrant professionals in the City: Local encounters, identities and inequalities.* New York: Routledge.

Meyer, J.-B. (2001). Network approach versus brain drain: Lessons from the diaspora. *International Migration, 39*(5), 91–110.

Paár-Jákli, G. (2014). *Networked governance and transatlantic relations: Building bridges through science diplomacy.* New York: Routledge.

Portes, A., Guarnizo, L., & Landolt, P. (2003). *La Globalización Desde Abajo: Transnacionalismo Inmigrante y Desarrollo: La Experiencia de Estados Unidos y América Latina.* Flacso México.

Reitz, J. G. (2005). Tapping immigrants' skills: New directions for Canadian immigration policy in the knowledge economy. *Law & Business Review of the Americas, 11*, 409.

Reitz, J. G., Banerjee, R., Phan, M., & Thompson, J. (2009). Race, religion, and the social integration of new immigrant minorities in Canada 1. *International Migration Review, 43*(4), 695–726.

Rutten, M., & Verstappen, S. (2014). Middling migration: Contradictory mobility experiences of Indian youth in London. *Journal of Ethnic and Migration Studies, 40*(8), 1217–1235.

Sapeha, H. (2015). Explaining variations in immigrants' satisfaction with their settlement experience. *Journal of International Migration and Integration, 16*(4), 891–910.

Sassen, S. (1999). *Globalization and Its Discontents: Essays on the New Mobility of People and Money.* http://www.citeulike.org/group/1128/article/631023

Schmidt, V. A. (2002). Does discourse matter in the politics of welfare state adjustment? *Comparative Political Studies, 35*(2), 168–193.

Siekierski, P., Lima, M. C., & Borini, F. M. (2018). International mobility of academics: Brain drain and brain gain. *European Management Review, 15*(3), 329–339. https://doi.org/10.1111/emre.12170.

Smith, M. P., & Favell, A. (2006). *The human face of global mobility: International highly skilled Migartion in Europe, North America and the Asia-Pacific* (Vol. 8). New Brunswick: Transaction Publishers.

Sumption, M., & Hu, X. (2011, July 1). *Scientists, managers, and tourists: The changing shape of European mobility to the United States.* Migrationpolicy.Org. https://www.migrationpolicy.org/research/european-migration-to-united-states

Torpey, J. (2000). *The Invention of the Passport: Surveillance, Citizenship and the State*. Cambridge University Press. http://books.google.it/books?hl=en&lr=&id=5vBtAgaFh6EC&oi=fnd&pg= PR9&dq=aristide+zolberg&ots=Ar3hlmiK5c&sig=Ff9JOL1I7V7iNL5C3j96uNv3NBY

Van Bouwel, L. (2010). "Return rates of European graduate students in the US: How many and who return, and when ?" *Belgeo. Revue Belge de Géographie, 4*(December), 395–405. https:// doi.org/10.4000/belgeo.7094.

Versailles, D. W., & Mérindol, V. (2006). Knowledge transfers and R&D management: An inquiry into the problem of transatlantic complementarities. *Defence and Peace Economics, 17*(3), 239–256.

Veugelers, R., & Cassiman, B. (2004). Foreign subsidiaries as a channel of international technology diffusion: Some direct firm level evidence from Belgium. *European Economic Review, 48*(2), 455–476.

Weinar, A. (2017). From emigrants to free movers: Whither European emigration and diaspora policy? *Journal of Ethnic and Migration Studies*, 1–19.

Weinar, Agnieszka. 2019. European citizenship and identity outside of the European Union. London/New York: Routledge.

Weinar, A., Desiderio, M. V., & Thibos, C. (2017). Governance of integration and the role of the countries of origin–a global perspective. In *Migrant integration between homeland and host society volume 1* (pp. 225–251). Cham: Springer.

Chapter 5
Conclusions

In this Reader we set out to present the growing research field on highly skilled migrants, which has shifted over the years from a clear distinction between migrants from the world's poorer countries and corporate expatriates from the world's wealthier countries to a more nuanced understanding of the wide variety of capital which each highly skilled migrant brings with him- or herself, regardless of country of origin or visa status. We started out from the premise that highly-skilled migrants are one group of migrants which is rarely politicized or seen in a negative light, whether in political or in public discourse, and examined the nuance in the concept and phenomenon of the contemporary highly skilled migrant. We noted that the discourse surrounding them perpetuates an image of high-earners with needed skills, who integrate easily and quickly. This perception makes them a "wanted" migration flow (Triadafilopoulos 2013). However, as with most migration flows, there is quite some distance between the popular perceptions of this migration flow and the more nuanced picture uncovered by social research. The objective of this Reader was to provide a basic understanding of the migration of the highly-skilled, but also to raise questions and to contribute to closing the divide between popular perception and research-based findings.

More specifically, we focused on the many gaps and contradictions interwoven into this research field. They can be divided into three broad groups of issues: conceptualisation and definition; integration patterns; mobility patterns. The most salient issue in the literature we examined is how the North-South divide is perpetuated in the field of study, and how it shapes, in an iterative way, the debates about these three groups of issues. Assumptions, perceptions and conceptualisations change according to what migrant we are discussing: a migrant from the Global North or the Global South; what state policy we are analysing: immigration or emigration policy. The different results for different sub-groups of the seemingly same highly skilled migrant category are stunning. They are also important to be aware of, so that future research employs more aware and more methodologically sound approaches to highly skilled migrants. At the same time, we also emphasize that the

© The Author(s) 2020
A. Weinar, A. Klekowski von Koppenfels, *Highly-Skilled Migration:
Between Settlement and Mobility*, IMISCOE Research Series,
https://doi.org/10.1007/978-3-030-42204-2_5

ongoing use of the term 'expatriates' to refer to all migrants from the Global North is a misnomer, and, moreover, one which leads to continuing misperceptions (cf. Klekowski von Koppenfels 2014, 2016).

5.1 Definitions

As we have shown in Chap. 2, the definitions of the highly skilled vary, and terminology used in literature to describe certain sub-categories varies as well.

Definitions of highly skilled have been proposed predominantly in the research that informs public policy, produced mainly in economics and political science. Hence, they have been driven by the administrative data, where the definitions are decided by policy makers, usually in the immigration policy field. In this light, highly skilled migrants are those who qualify for highly skilled immigration schemes and are thus captured in data by specific immigration channels. These policy-centered approaches use the concepts of educational attainment and skill level to define their target group. Some use these two indicators together with salary as an additional measure. All three are defined in nominal terms, based on official aggregated databases and have been used by economists and policy scholars to support policymakers when designing or evaluating their immigration policies. However, what seemed straightforward two decades ago is now a contested approach.

As regards the first notion in "highly skilled migrant", the "highly," the commonly applied cut-off at tertiary education conflates "highly skilled" with "highly educated." Scholars argue that educational attainment is not reflective of highly skilled in the real world, either because the definition of tertiary educated differs from country to country, it comprises several levels of education (e.g. a college degree vs PhD), or because low-skilled migrants can come to the country of destination to complete tertiary education that qualifies them for the highly skilled label. Moreover, the quality of tertiary education differs across the world, and the educational attainment is not synonymous with skills needed on the labour market. The implied difference in quality of education and training between the North and South educational systems underpins the divide. Similarly, there are many other groups that move internationally outside of the highly skilled migration channels, but whose educational attainment might fit the bill of a highly skilled migrant: these are students, migrant dependants (usually spouses) and refugees. So far, the least problematic group of these three are international students, who are treated by many governments and scholars alike as highly skilled migrants-to-be. However, researchers have also drawn our attention to the fact that spouses or refugees are often skilled migrants, but ones whose skills are not given enough credit at destination. Moreover, the phenomenon of knowledge migration blurs the categories, when dependants and refugees alike attend tertiary education institutions and become students, either international or domestic.

The discussion on educational attainment has led to the new debate on the meaning of "skill" in "highly skilled migrant." Is tertiary education always equivalent to skills? The overarching pressure on states to participate in the global "race for talent" only exacerbates the problem. As many scholars have argued, "skill" or "talent" is often not measurable in an objective way. Skills and talent are context-dependent and are different from one economy to the next. There are various skill requirements, varying through sectors and labour markets in the countries of destination, and different skills are valued in different societies. Researchers have brought to light the importance of practical, cross-sector skill sets that can be taught in one educational and social system, but not in another. It is also clear that economies will need different skill levels, ranging from sophisticated trade skills to postdoctoral level skills in narrow disciplines. What constitutes a skill or talent is thus decided by the policymakers who design specific recruitment programs. This does then mean that it is impossible to offer a universal definition.

Finally, the notion of "migrant" in "highly skilled migrant" has also been contested. As many scholars have noted, the widely accepted UN definition of an "international migrant" is a person who resides in another country for longer than 12 months. However, many highly skilled migrants engage in circular or temporary migration, under 12 months. The administrative data collection systems are usually geared towards the long-term definition. It means that they do not necessarily capture and take into account the temporary flows. Moreover, the core and traditional idea of a "migrant", coined in the classic studies of Transatlantic migrations of the past century and lingering to this day in the popular imagination, is that they are a permanent presence, migrating for settlement. Alas, in the modern connected economy, highly skilled migrants with internationally marketable skills (this, on the other hand, is a notion defined by global companies, not policymakers) are very mobile. This concerns such different groups as researchers, managers, technicians or creative professionals. As they move frequently beyond the immigration schemes and rather under the GATS IV provisions, they are often not considered migrants.

This group has been researched by the scholars of business management studies. The longstanding interest in the classic "organisational expatriate," the constant feature of the global economic system from the 1980s well into the early 2000s, brought about a rich academic research. However, recently scholars have argued for the needed expansion of the field. Indeed, Further work of consolidating the definition and building reliable **interdisciplinary** taxonomies is crucial for the development of this research field. For the moment many disciplines use many definitions and they often do not talk to each other.

5.2 Integration of the Highly Skilled

In contrast to the lower-skilled, a primary objective of policies focusing on attracting highly skilled migrants is, more often than not, to encourage them to stay. However, since this group of migrants is more prone to mobility than lesser-skilled groups, not only because of their educational background, but also the global opportunity structure for their skills, this objective and their profile come into conflict. Therefore the central question from an employer-centred policy approach is: how to make highly skilled migrants stay and settle? Interestingly enough, the question of retention is important both for the countries of origin and destination: the first interested in attenuating brain drain and maximise brain gain effects, while the latter trying to improve the economic impact of immigration and investment in integration. Consequently, the scholarly interest in integration patterns has grown substantially over recent years and there has been a wealth of literature approaching this question. There are five takeaways of all research in this field so far. First, we noted that sociologists and anthropologists are leading the research into integration of highly skilled migrants, but there are very few political scientists who engage in this field.

Second, we observed that qualitative micro-studies of small samples of immigrants are most commonly showcased, while there are very few large-scale qualitative surveys of these migrants.

Third, labour market/professional integration seems to be the dominant theme; however there is an emerging discussion on a variety of integration challenges of the highly skilled, which shows that they are increasingly viewed as just migrants.

Fourth, and as a consequence of the first observation, cultural capital (social skills and professional skills) is the often-used lens of this analysis. Bourdieusian capital is a part of the internalised baggage of each migrant. During migration tensions arise from the fact that host society puts "country labels" on each individual and their cultural capital. This is an important factor of integration on the labour market, the key element of the decision to settle for the highly skilled. In fact, the highly skilled are at most risk of employment below their skill level and loss of status, which also seem to be exacerbated by female gender (Gauthier 2016; Adamuti-Trache 2011; Purkayastha 2005). The less value cultural capital has in the eyes of the host society, the more painful adjustment trajectories might become. Scholars have noted that often Global Northerners have an easier access to the labour market because of the lower hard and soft barriers to their integration. On the macro level, state cooperation that creates specific opportunity structures, such as enhanced mobility or easier work permit procedures (hard berries), as well as an easier recognition of qualifications (soft barriers). On meso-level they can enjoy professional networks created thanks to enhanced mobility and language skills, and generally a superior opinion as regards their skills and work values. These are the "country labels" at work. We have noted that Southerners might encounter more hard and soft barriers to labour market integration on these two levels, with less opportunity structures and more in-built bias.

Fifth, there is a strand of literature dealing with the integration of the specific category of highly skilled that can be defined as organisational expatriates. They are usually studied as not really in need of integration; Marouk refers to them as "accidental tourists". There are also no expectations of their integration and their situation has been described as a constant tension between exclusion and inclusion (van Bochove and Engbersen 2015). The fact that for many years this type of migrant dominated the literature had adverse effects on studies of highly skilled in non-expatriate situations, especially, but not only, when coming from the Global South. As this Reader has discussed, the breadth of highly skilled migrants, as well as migrants from the Global North, cannot be limited to the term organisational expatriate. We hope the complexity of the category of the highly skilled migrant has been demonstrated in this Reader.

Sixth, we concluded that integration support in host countries usually focuses on the most vulnerable migrants, who are most often defined by skill level – by being low-skilled. Apart from very few countries (Canada and Australia), highly skilled are believed to be able to find their way to the satisfying future. The negative effects of failed labour market integration can be felt for generations. This is particularly important when we look at highly skilled migrant as an empowered actor, constantly making decisions about their lives and professional development. The way they negotiate the soft barriers to labour market integration may vary depending on each individual situation and capital brought along.

And finally, in our review, we saw that gendered analysis of integration patterns of the highly skilled migrants brings to front the additional obstacles that migrants, especially women, face when pursuing a professional career while migrating internationally. A complex set of tensions between societies of origin and destination, and the individual stance of an empowered migrant brings about a variety of challenges to integration on several levels.

One theme that is common to all these accounts is that highly skilled migrants, even if unsuccessful in their migration project, are still empowered. They are not victims of a global system, but rather they are (often) able to be actors, and in control of their own destiny – however, it is clear that their efforts may nonetheless go wrong for external reasons. It is also clear that many low-skilled migrants are equally able to make independent decisions concerning their migration projects, but as we have demonstrated throughout this Reader, the highly skilled simply have more options for migration. Taking the perspective of the highly skilled migrant into account helps us understand why many of them would stay, even if faced with less than ideal professional pathways in the destination country, and helps us understand why some would move once again regardless of their professional success in the destination country. Elements of integration that are less directly focused on careers, such as lifestyle, urban environment (e.g. Global City), security or simply family dynamics (professional satisfaction for the spouse), are all important elements of migrants' decision-making. In general, there is still not much literature on these factors not directly related to employment on-professional factors of integration among highly skilled migrants; to have a stronger and more nuanced approach to integration, future research could draw on such aspects as well. The past and current research has been rather focused on the Global Northerners or on Chinese or Indian migrants, and this includes many studies on student migration. The research area is definitely underdeveloped and needs stronger analytical focus to be able to bring all available microstudies and present a coherent narrative on the integration pathways of the highly skilled, as it exists for the low skilled migrants.

5.3   Mobility Patterns

Highly skilled migrants are not restricted to any one global region. Literature has
shown growing interest in this type of migration occurring in all directions: South-
North, North-North, North-South and South-South (the latter is understudied). For
the most part, South-North mobility is approached as long-term, permanent migration. Although there is evidence that South-North mobility of the highly skilled can
also be short-term and temporary, still the prevalent discourse in the literature is
about highly skilled immigration from developing to developed countries. On the
other end of the spectrum lies North-South mobility, with short-term posted migrant
workers seen as essential mobile non-migrants. In this context, North-North migrations are in-between. They give us a hint to the future of the highly skilled migration
patterns more globally.

Drivers of mobility in the transatlantic migration system are related to economic
and political cooperation that has developed in this area over the last (twentieth)
century. The transatlantic migration system is organised by state power networks
that regulate mobilities of citizens within them and thus the ascent of the European
Union with its bold ideas of open borders for goods, services and people has influenced the bilateral policies across the Atlantic. The idea of beneficial influence of
people-to-people contacts and profits brought by mobility of certain workers to the
transnational businesses has shaped the transatlantic space as we know it today: it
went from closed to semi-open space for migrants with the right passports. 100 years
ago, poor Europeans were flocking to the Ellis Island in search of better lives, while
poor American artists wanted to make it in Paris and return. Tables have turned and
it is the temporary mobility of the highly skilled which dominates the transatlantic
space nowadays. They cross the Atlantic in both directions, in different ways: as
economic immigrants, as temporary visitors, as service providers, as students and as
spouses/partners. They use available opportunity structures and enjoy lower risk
mobility for professional or individual development. If they decide to settle, it is
often because of their consideration of the specific context: lifestyle, professional
opportunities. The classic ideas of wage differentials are no longer a decisive factor
shaping the decision to stay. Moreover, even if settled for several years or more, the
transatlantic migrants are prone to secondary migrations, return or forward. This
extreme mobility reflects the future of all global migrations.

5.4   Direction of Further Research

The field of highly skilled migration studies continues to evolve rapidly. It is a challenging field considering limited official data and the wide range of conceptualisations. When there is not any one stable definition, as is the case here, the object of
study moves constantly, and changes from scholar to scholar. There is a disconnect

between academic disciplines when studying highly skilled migrants; interdisciplinarity is a challenge with respected to the highly-skilled.

There are several emerging themes that in our view could be further explored when researching highly skilled migrants:

- highly skilled mobility from the Global South – how much can this type of mobility tell us about the assumed particularity and privilege of highly skilled migrants in general? There is a need for more critical and more bias-conscious study of highly skilled flows, even using the administrative data in big quantitative sets.
- large-scale qualitative studies, which would allow for group cross-comparison in various receiving contexts.
- More research into the multiple mobility among the skilled and highly skilled migrants which would allow for a redefinition of what migration is in the twenty-first century. We firmly believe that increased mobility, as opposed to settlement, is the phenomenon at play, for a variety of reasons.
- Large scale qualitative and quantitative studies of opportunity structures that enhance international mobility beyond immigration programs.
- More nuanced research into the role of family members as skilled migrants in their own right, including an increased focus on same-sex couples.
- Increasing research into migrants from the Global North, their reasons for migration, and their patterns of mobility.

One thing is certain: as we are in the early stages, the future of research on highly skilled migration looks promising and exciting. As the world around us evolves, the knowledge transfers become crucial for stability and prosperity of the globe, and our understanding of it changes, the highly skilled migrant will become a more important object of study in the years to come.

References

Adamuti-Trache, M. (2011). First 4 years in Canada: Post-secondary education pathways of highly educated immigrants. *Journal of International Migration and Integration/Revue de l'integration et de La Migration Internationale, 12*(1), 61–83.

Gauthier, C.-A. (2016). Obstacles to socioeconomic integration of highly-skilled immigrant women: Lessons from Quebec Interculturalism and implications for diversity management. *Equality, Diversity and Inclusion: An International Journal, 35*(1), 17–30.

Klekowski von Koppenfels, A. (2014). *Migrants or expatriates?: Americans in Europe*. New York: Springer.

Purkayastha, B. (2005). Skilled migration and cumulative disadvantage: The case of highly qualified Asian Indian immigrant women in the US. *Geoforum, 36*(2), 181–196.

Triadafilopoulos, T. (2013). *Wanted and welcome?: Policies for highly skilled immigrants in comparative perspective*. New York: Springer Science & Business Media.

van Bochove, M., & Engbersen, G. (2015). Beyond cosmopolitanism and expat bubbles: Challenging dominant representations of knowledge workers and trailing spouses. *Population Space and Place, 21*(4), 295–309.